Also by Dr. Phil McGraw

*The Ultimate Weight Solution Food Guide*

*The Ultimate Weight Solution*

*The Self Matters Companion*

*Self Matters*

*Relationship Rescue Workbook*

*Relationship Rescue*

*Life Strategies Workbook*

*Life Strategies*

# The Ultimate Weight Solution Cookbook

## Recipes for Weight Loss Freedom

# Dr. Phil McGraw

Free Press

New York   London   Toronto   Sydney

*f*P

FREE PRESS
A Division of Simon & Schuster, Inc.
1230 Avenue of the Americas
New York, NY 10020

Copyright © 2004 by Phillip C. McGraw
All rights reserved,
including the right of reproduction
in whole or in part in any form.

FREE PRESS and colophon are trademarks
of Simon & Schuster, Inc.

For information about special discounts for bulk purchases,
please contact Simon & Schuster Special Sales:
1-800-456-6798 or business@simonandschuster.com

Designed by Charles Kreloff
Photographs by Lou Manna

Manufactured in the United States of America

10   9   8   7   6   5   4   3   2   1

Library of Congress Control Number: 2004047052

ISBN 0-7432-6475-4

This book is dedicated to the millions of people who are using *The Ultimate Weight Solution* and changing the epidemic of obesity in America, one life at a time.

# Acknowledgments

The crusade of tackling obesity in America has been my passion. The more information I can put in your hands to help you take back control of your weight the more likely you will find the weight loss freedom you have been craving. When I decided to put together this cookbook, I amassed a team of only the best whose talents and expertise could help me create more tools for your journey to health and wellness.

Thanks to Maggie Robinson, Ph.D., the most exemplary nutritional consultant in America today. Your unsurpassed knowledge of nutritional science has been an invaluable asset not only to me, but to the insurmountable number of readers who have attained their goal with *The Ultimate Weight Solution*.

Thanks to Judy Kern, Project Manager, for being the unswerving shepherd of the plan. Your commitment to get things done right has made this book all the more lip-smacking good.

Thanks to Bruce Weinstein and Mark Scarbrough for your dedication to the innovation, assembly, and testing of my favorite recipes.

My appreciation also to Dominick Anfuso for his tireless efforts to create a cookbook as beautiful as it is helpful to its reader. Truly, beauty is in the eye of the beholder, and Dominick, your eye is keen!

# Contents

# Introduction

The more tools I can put in your hands to help you manage your weight, the better the job you will do at creating a life defined by health and vitality. Now, with *The Ultimate Weight Solution Cookbook,* you have the latest in a set of tools designed to help you improve your way of eating, achieve a healthier weight, feel better, and experience far greater energy—and make all these changes for life.

Millions of you have already taken steps in that direction by acquiring *The Ultimate Weight Solution: The 7 Keys to Weight Loss Freedom,* and its companion, *The Ultimate Weight Solution Food Guide.* Everything in those two books equips and empowers you to do the work of changing your lifestyle, becoming the healthy, fit person you were meant to be, and, ultimately, maximizing your life and everything you have to give.

Since *The Ultimate Weight Solution* was published, I have been both humbled and inspired by the sustainable, life-altering results people are achieving with regard to weight management and better health. On average, the results that come from learning and applying the seven keys have produced dramatic weight losses.

There is, however, much more to the story than that. As the numbers on these people's scales fell steadily from week to week, so did other critical numbers including LDL cholesterol and triglyceride levels, blood pressure, and blood sugar. Once indicative of declining health and an early skid into the cemetery, these lowered levels began to reflect a new vibrancy of recharged health.

As people internalized the seven keys, making them a part of their deepest self, they began to live a new life with a rock-solid foundation that no shifting circumstance or disappointment will be able destroy. These are people who got real with themselves, for themselves. They did not do it with willpower or intentions, but with action, courage, and commitment.

If you are one of these success stories, I am thrilled for you and your achievement. If you are not—if you are barely treading water with yet another diet—then today, at this very moment, let the words on these pages become a wake-up call, because I do not want you to go through one more hour or one more day drowning in misery or headed for more of the same. This very day you can begin to make a difference in your life. All you have to do is open your hands, firmly grasp all the tools available to you, including this cookbook, and use them.

I confess that, with the exception of firing up my grill for barbecues (it is a requirement of Life 101 for Texans to master the art of outdoor grilling), I don't do a whole lot of cooking. And so, for *The Ultimate Weight Solution Cookbook,* I brought together an innovative and expert cast of culinary and nutrition experts to develop these recipes, many of which were inspired by our family's favorite foods. This remarkable team collaborated with me and Robin, my wife of twenty-eight years, and put together some of the healthiest and most delicious meals possible. Together, we tested every recipe to ensure that it tasted great and offered high-level nutrition that would help you manage your weight and put health and vitality back into your life.

If you have resolved to cook lighter, leaner, and smarter this year and in the years ahead, you have come to the right place. Designed to work with the food plans in *The Ultimate Weight So-*

*lution* and *The Ultimate Weight Solution Food Guide,* the recipes in this book use a wide variety of wholesome, nutrient-rich foods that will move your weight and your health in a better direction. With these recipes, you will produce meals that taste better and cost less, and you will avoid the overload of refined carbohydrates, saturated fats, salt, and sugars that are ruining your waistline and your health.

At the same time, these recipes are full of so much flavor that they are destined to become standards in your mealtime repertoire. This should be welcome news if you have ever become bored with healthy food choices and abandoned your weight-control efforts because of it. Every recipe is designed to help you succeed at keeping your weight in line without giving up the tastes you love.

You will not find any recipes here that enslave you to the kitchen for endless hours, because in today's rush of the world, there seems to be less and less time for cooking and food preparation. Our recipes take only a minimum of preparation time, so that you will be able to spend less, rather than more, time in your kitchen.

Nor will you find skimpy diet-type meals that taste like wallpaper paste. I wanted the recipes in this book to be not only nutritious but also hearty and filling, stick-to-your-ribs meals that you will want to prepare and enjoy again and again.

A self-defeating mistake made by many people who decide to lose weight is to prepare one meal (a diet meal) for themselves and an entirely different meal, one that is infinitely more fattening, for their families. How inconvenient, ridiculous, and depriving is that! Not to mention a disservice to their families. I'm betting that if you have done this, you are so tempted so much of the time, just by having to handle and prepare stuff that probably shouldn't be in your kitchen anyway, that you cave in to the temptation, put on your what's-the-use face, and overindulge with everyone else. And so, you're back to square one, as another attempt to lose weight bites the dust.

That kind of self-defeating behavior stops here, and it stops now. Our recipes have been created for your entire family to enjoy, whether or not they need to shed pounds. No longer will you be required to fix one meal for yourself and another for the rest of your family. No, these are meals for everyone. When you make them a part of your everyday cooking, you will be taking care of yourself while at the same time taking care of your kids, your spouse, and everyone else you love.

As I have often said, you do not *need* to lose weight or become healthier—you *deserve* to do it. Using *The Ultimate Weight Solution* books as your guides, you now have one of the best opportunities you'll ever have to lose weight. That's a great deal—having the opportunity to enhance your life. But let me repeat myself for emphasis: I'm not just saying that you *need* to do it; I'm saying you *deserve* to do it. You deserve something better for your life, and now is the moment to go after it. Let these books move you forward on your journey to weight loss freedom.

It is my hope, and Robin's hope, that this cookbook will become a welcome resource in your household for nutritious, healthy, and delicious meals that you and your family can enjoy both today and in the future. As you turn the pages, we invite you to share with us some of our very own favorite foods and our favorite ways of preparing them. So from our kitchen—and our home—to yours . . . enjoy!

DR. PHIL AND ROBIN MCGRAW

# PART ONE

# Getting Started

# 1 Cooking the Ultimate Weight Solution Way

Listen, you can get down to size in the coming months, but you have to be different and do different—right down to the way you cook. At first, it can be difficult, indeed a challenge, to weaken the grip of any habit, and old cooking habits are no different. When you think about some of your own cooking habits, such as frying foods, baking desserts, and cooking with a lot of sugar and fat, and you see how they are perpetuating your weight problem, you'll understand that you need to get rid of them; you need to change those habits.

In cooking, the change can be as simple as making a few ingredient substitutions, learning how to use spices and seasonings in new ways, or changing your cooking methods so that less fat or sugar is required. As you become nutritionally more aware, you'll discover that you can still cook most of your favorite recipes as long as you are open to making small and subtle adjustments in how you do things. The bottom line is that you must adjust your behavior so that you are willing to try some new techniques, leaving behind the old and the familiar. This cookbook will be right here to guide you as you do that.

Once you put a whole new way of cooking, one that will put you in control of your weight, at the top of your priority list— call it a *new track to run on*—this healthier way of cooking will become a part of your total health picture and your lifestyle. In fact, you'll begin to wonder why you didn't start cooking like this a long time ago. So, promise yourself now that you'll care enough about your weight and your health to do this—and do it right!

# Foods to Look for: High-Response Cost, High-Yield Foods

The recipes created for you in this cookbook are designed around nutrient-dense, hunger-curbing foods that I call *high-response cost, high-yield foods. High-response* means that the effort on your part, or *response*, that is required to prepare, chew, and ingest these foods is high, whereas the calorie payoff—although healthy—is low.

High-response cost foods take longer to eat, and thus encourage slower eating (a positive habit that is important to long-term weight control). These foods are *hunger suppressors*, meaning they produce *satisfaction*, the feeling of normal fullness you look for from a meal. From the perspective of weight management, high-response cost, high-yield foods support behavioral change. They encourage better eating habits, they are tremendously satisfying, they curb cravings and hunger pangs, and they defeat impulse eating.

What are some examples of high-response cost foods? In general, they include fresh fruits and vegetables, whole grains, lean proteins, dairy products, and healthy fats and oils. Take an apple, for example. It is coarse and takes a lot of chewing and grinding on your part to get it down. And it's also packed with fiber, which keeps your stomach from emptying too rapidly.

Most high-response cost foods also happen to be high-yield foods. *High-yield foods* are those that supply a lot of nutrients, in the form of carbohydrates, protein, fat, vitamins, minerals, fiber, phytonutrients, and other food components, relative to the low amount of calories they contain.

Look for more ways to include high-response cost, high-yield foods in your daily diet and you will increase your chances of success. (For a list of all the high-response cost, high-yield foods you can enjoy on my food plans, please refer to pages 150–417 of *The Ultimate Weight Solution Food Guide.*)

# Foods to Limit or Avoid: Low-Response Cost, Low-Yield Foods

If you want the pounds to begin dropping away, there is a category of foods you must push yourself to limit or avoid altogether: low-response, low-yield foods. These foods require very little effort, or *response*, from you when you eat them. In plain terms, they are foods you just gulp and gain from—quickly ingested, too convenient, requiring little or no preparation on your part. Junk foods, candy, convenience foods, and certain fast foods are all examples of low-response cost, low-yield foods.

Overindulging in low-response cost, low-yield foods can send you on a bullet train to becoming overweight and, potentially, obese because they lead to a considerable amount of mindless, uncontrollable overeating. When you eliminate or cut back on these foods, weight management becomes much easier and requires far less vigilance over what and how you eat.

Most low-response cost foods are also *low-yield foods*. That means they provide very little in the way of good nutrition or fiber, with a huge number of calories packed into a very small amount of food. What's more, they are processed and refined; that is, they have been altered in some fashion that devalues their nutrition by extracting fiber and other nutrients. They can make your body feel so physically imbalanced that, as a result, you often experience fatigue and low energy.

One of the most sabotaging aspects of low-response cost, low-yield foods is that they are *hunger drivers*. They do not keep you satisfied for very long and may make you even hungrier later. Here's why: You eat them so quickly that your body's natural stop-eating signals don't have time to kick in. So, you keep eating more and more of this stuff until you've eaten way beyond the point of fullness, and the unfortunate fact is that you're overfed with unnecessary calories and fat. (For a full list of low-response cost, low-yield foods, refer to pages 418–707 of *The Ultimate Weight Solution Food Guide*.)

# A Three-Stage Plan to Weight-Loss Freedom

For those of you who have not yet read *The Ultimate Weight Solution* or *The Ultimate Weight Solution Food Guide* or who are reading it now, I want to provide you with an overview of the nutritional plan set forth in these books, broken down to the daily level of what to eat and when to eat it. This is not a fad diet that denies you the satisfaction of eating—one of our most basic drives—far from it. Nor does it require white-knuckle dieting. Because it includes such a wide range of satisfying high-response cost, high-yield foods, this plan provides a workable, sustainable three-stage plan for taking weight off and keeping it off.

## Stage 1: The Rapid Start Plan

To begin, you should follow this fourteen-day, calorie-controlled, carbohydrate-modified plan that helps your body gear up for accelerated weight loss, detoxes you from sugar and refined carbohydrates, and conditions your taste preferences for healthier foods. In addition, the weight loss you achieve within just fourteen days will give you the confidence boost you need to move on to the next two stages and the rest of what you need to do. Here is a typical day on the Rapid Start Plan:

| | |
|---|---|
| **Breakfast** | 1 protein serving (egg, egg whites; lean turkey ham or turkey bacon) |

1 starchy carbohydrate (whole-grain or high-fiber cereal)*

1 fruit (piece of fresh whole fruit)

1 low-fat dairy food (skim, low-fat, or soy milk; low-fat, sugar-free yogurt)

1 noncaloric beverage (coffee, tea)

---

**Lunch**

1 protein serving (lean meat, fish, poultry, or vegetarian protein such as tofu, legumes, or soy products)

2 nonstarchy vegetables (salad vegetables, broccoli, cauliflower, green beans, leafy vegetables, in virtually unlimited amounts)

1 fruit (piece of fresh whole fruit)

1 low-fat dairy food (skim, low-fat, or soy milk; low-fat, sugar-free yogurt)

1 noncaloric beverage (coffee, tea)

---

**Dinner**

1 protein serving (lean meat, fish, poultry, or vegetarian protein such as tofu, legumes, or soy products)

2 nonstarchy vegetables (salad vegetables, broccoli, cauliflower, green beans, leafy vegetables, in virtually unlimited amounts)

1 fat (1 tablespoon of any healthy fat such as olive oil, canola oil, or 2 tablespoons of a reduced-fat salad dressing, for example)

1 noncaloric beverage (coffee, tea)

---

**Snacks**

Fresh whole fruit, if not eaten with a meal

Low-fat dairy food, if not eaten with a meal

Raw vegetables

* Men: Add one starchy carbohydrate at lunch or dinner.

# Stage 2: The High-Response Cost, High-Yield Weight Loss Plan

Stage 2 creates greater metabolic control so that your body uses more calories for energy and stores fewer calories as fat. This is because the foods you will eat are low in sugar and refined carbohydrates, as opposed to high-fat, high-sugar foods that tend to promote weight gain when eaten in excess. By avoiding the wrong kinds of carbohydrates, namely sugary processed foods, you gain a tremendous edge in managing your weight. Here is a typical day on Stage 2:

| | |
|---|---|
| **Breakfast** | 1 protein serving (egg, egg whites; lean turkey ham or turkey bacon) |
| | 1 starchy carbohydrate (whole grain or high-fiber cereal; whole-wheat bread, roll, or muffin)* |
| | 1 fruit (piece of fresh whole fruit, ½ cup fruit canned in water or juice, 1 cup unsweetened fruit juice, or a serving of dried fruit)† |
| | 1 low-fat dairy food (skim, low-fat, or soy milk; low-fat, sugar-free yogurt) |
| | 1 noncaloric beverage (coffee, tea) |
| **Lunch** | 1 protein serving (lean meat, fish, poultry, or vegetarian protein such as tofu, legumes, or soy products) |
| | 2 nonstarchy vegetables (salad vegetables, broccoli, cauliflower, green beans, leafy vegetables, in virtually unlimited amounts) |
| | 1 starchy carbohydrate (brown rice or other whole grains; whole- |

*\* Men: Add one starchy carbohydrate at lunch or dinner.*
*† Refer to* The Ultimate Weight Solution Food Guide *for correct serving sizes of dried fruit.*

grain bread or cracker products; potato or sweet potato; beans
and legumes)

1 fruit (piece of fresh whole fruit, $1/2$ cup fruit canned in water or
juice, 1 cup unsweetened fruit juice, or a serving of dried fruit)*

1 low-fat dairy food (skim, low-fat, or soy milk; low-fat, sugar-free
yogurt; reduced-fat cheese)

1 noncaloric beverage (coffee, tea)

---

**Dinner**

1 protein serving (lean meat, fish, poultry, or vegetarian protein such
as tofu, legumes, or soy products)

2 or more nonstarchy vegetables (salad vegetables, broccoli,
cauliflower, green beans, leafy vegetables, in virtually unlimited
amounts)

1 fat (1 tablespoon of any healthy fat such as olive oil, canola oil, or
2 tablespoons of a reduced-fat salad dressing; 1 tablespoon of
nuts or seeds)

1 noncaloric beverage

---

**Snacks**

Fresh whole fruit, if not eaten with a meal

Low-fat dairy food, if not eaten with a meal

Raw vegetables

* Refer to The Ultimate Weight Solution Food Guide *for correct serving sizes of dried*
*fruit.*

# Stage 3: Ultimate Maintenance

Once you reach your ideal weight, you may liberalize the number of servings you eat of foods taken mainly from the high-response cost, high-yield list. Use the following daily serving allotments to assist in your food planning.

- Protein and protein substitutes: 3 servings
- Nonstarchy vegetables: as many as you like (don't skimp here)
- Starchy carbohydrates: 3 to 4 servings
- Fruits: 3 to 4 servings
- Low-fat dairy products: 2 to 3 servings
- Healthy fats: 1 to 2 servings

All the recipes you will find on the following pages can be folded into any of these three stages. By way of example, and to indicate just how much variety you can enjoy, at the end of this chapter I've provided a 14-day meal plan for the Rapid Start Plan that uses close to forty of the recipes in this book, making the challenges of life-long weight control easier for you to meet. The meal plan proves that you can quite literally feast your way to a trimmer body and make its health benefits an easy-to-maintain way of life.

In fact, when you eat and cook this way while following all seven keys to weight-loss freedom, you can expect to lose weight, and you will keep on losing weight steadily and satisfactorily as you stay on target for achieving your goal weight. It is also an excellent plan for lowering risk factors for chronic diseases, or as a way to simply feel better and experience far greater energy. (I've summarized the seven keys for you on pages 16–17.)

# Using the Ultimate Weight Solution Recipes

As you map out your menus, commit yourself to checking the *nutrient analysis* at the end of each recipe. Each analysis includes values for calories, protein, carbohydrate, total fat, saturated fat, cholesterol, fiber, sugar, and sodium—all information that is relevant to lifetime weight control and good health. Although I am not a fan of counting calories, calculating carbohydrate or fat grams, or multiplying nutrient percentages, I do believe that monitoring these nutrients from time to time is an effective way to keep yourself accountable and progress steadily toward your goals.

Unless otherwise specified, each analysis is based on a single serving. There is also a note at the end of each analysis that explains whether the serving counts as a protein, nonstarchy vegetable, starchy carbohydrate, fruit, low-fat dairy product, fat, or some combination of these. This is all valuable information you can use in your meal planning.

Very often, the recipes use a scant amount of healthy fat, low-fat dairy products, starchy carbohydrate, or egg, mainly for flavor and texture. The amount used is so negligible that you do not have to count it toward your fat, dairy, carbohydrate, or protein servings for the day. In addition, a number of free foods have been used to create many of the recipes. *Free foods* are very low in calories and carbohydrates per serving and include fat-free or sugar-free foods, such as fat-free cream cheese, fat-free sour cream, sugar-free pudding mix, or sugar-free gelatin desserts.

The serving sizes for each recipe approximate the amount you should eat at your meals. Staying mindful of your serving sizes can make all the difference in the world when it comes to

losing, gaining, or maintaining your weight and is thus funda-
mentally important in successful weight management.

Of course, the larger the portion, the more calories it contains. Further, research has proven time and time again that serving large portions encourages people to eat more. It is simply a
fact of eating behavior that people will eat what is put in front of
them. If more food is there, they will eat more food.

If you are unsure of exactly how much to eat, here is a useful
chart that defines for you exactly what healthy, sensible portions
should look like. Use this information to determine the size and
amount of your portions when you eat at home as well as when
you dine out.

| Food | Portion Size |
|---|---|
| **Meat, fish, or poultry** | Size of the palm of your hand, your computer mouse, or a deck of cards |
| **Vegetables** | |
| Raw | Size of your fist |
| Cooked | Size of your hand when cupped |
| **Starchy carbohydrates** | |
| Cereal and cooked grains | Size of your hand when cupped |
| Bread | 1 slice, or the size of a computer disk |
| Bagel | 1/2 bagel |
| English muffin | 1/2 English muffin |
| Muffin | 1 cupcake wrapper |
| Crackers | Number of crackers listed in the recipe per serving or the food guide |
| Legumes and other starchy vegetables | Size of your hand when cupped |
| **Fruit** | |
| Raw piece | Size of a tennis ball |
| Canned (in water or juice), or frozen | Size of your hand when cupped |
| Berries (raw or frozen), raw chopped fruit | Size of your fist |
| **Dairy foods** | |
| Milk and yogurt | Size of your fist |
| Cottage cheese | Size of your hand when cupped |
| Cheese | Size of a pair of dice |
| Sandwich cheese | 1 slice, or the size of a computer disk |
| **1 tablespoon of fats, oils, salad dressings, or nuts and seeds** | Size of your thumb to the first joint, a teabag, or a walnut |

# You Can Succeed

Whatever your earlier diet experiences have been, you now have a second chance. You can shape your life around who you really are and what really defines you and matters to you, and your weight is certainly something in your life that you want to change.

Taking the journey toward weight loss freedom requires a willing spirit—and a commitment—to try something new for a change, and for a change in *you*. By reading this book, by using its recipes, by opening your mind to the possibility of a better, healthier lifestyle, you are making a difference this very day.

# The 7 Keys to Weight Loss Freedom

### Key #1: Right thinking.

Lay aside self-defeating, invalid mindsets that do not work. They have the power to keep you from making different choices or developing new behaviors. Too often, we let these negative notions go unchallenged, and act as if they were true. You must monitor what you're thinking and challenge its truth. If it's not working, replace it with thinking that works.

### Key #2: Healing feelings.

Overcome emotional overeating by managing inappropriate reactions to stress; solve problems rather than dwelling on them; change self-defeating thoughts, since, more often than not, feelings follow thoughts; gain closure on unfinished emotional business; and learn new ways to cope without resorting to food.

### Key #3: A No-fail environment.

Design your world so that you can't help succeeding. This involves removing temptations to eat and rearranging your schedule in order to avoid or minimize triggers to overeat.

### Key #4: Mastery over food and impulse eating.

There's only one reason why you haven't changed the bad stuff in your life. You're getting something out of it. I'm not saying that you're getting something healthy or positive, but people do not continue in situations, attitudes, or actions that do not give them a payoff. This key helps you identify those payoffs, unplug from them, and replace bad habits with healthy behavior.

### Key #5: High-response, high-yield nutrition.

To lose weight, you must choose foods that support good behavioral control over your eating; that is, high-response cost, high-yield foods, organized into a moderate, balanced, calorie-controlled plan to ensure weight loss.

### Key #6: Intentional exercise.

Make regular exercise a priority in your life most days of the week: walking, jogging, aerobic dance classes, yoga, playing a sport, or lifting weights. Exercise does more than simply burn calories; it changes your self-perception so that you stop labeling yourself a couch potato.

### Key #7: Your circle of support.

Surround yourself with supportive, like-minded people who want you to lose weight and succeed at your health and fitness efforts.

# The Rapid Start 14-Day Menu Plan

## Day 1

| | |
|---|---|
| **Breakfast** | 1 serving *Chili Cheddar Grits* (page 67)<br>1 cup low-fat milk<br>1 egg (or two egg whites), scrambled<br>1 cup strawberries (or other fresh seasonal fruit)<br>Coffee or tea |
| **Snack** | 1 cup low-fat, sugar-free plain yogurt mixed with 1 tablespoon<br>    sugar-free apricot preserves |
| **Lunch** | 1 serving *Seared Tuna Salad* (page 83)<br>Fresh pear |
| **Snack** | 1 serving *Guacamole* (page 168) with raw cut-up vegetables |
| **Dinner** | 1 serving *Herb Roasted Chicken* (page 116)<br>1 serving *Asparagus with a Warm Vinaigrette* (page 157)<br>Summer squash (crookneck), steamed or boiled |

*Daily Nutrition Profile:* 1,200 calories; 110 g protein; 133 g carbohydrate; 30 g total fat; 5 g saturated fat; 380 mg cholesterol; 20 g fiber; 1 g sugar; 2,515 mg sodium

# Day 2

| | |
|---|---|
| **Breakfast** | 1 serving *Tex-Mex Scramble* (page 58)<br>1 *Refrigerator Applesauce Bran Muffin* (page 70)<br>¹/₂ grapefruit<br>Coffee or tea |

| | |
|---|---|
| **Snack** | Banana smoothie: 1 frozen banana blended with 1 cup low-fat milk or soy milk and artificial sweetener (optional) |

| | |
|---|---|
| **Lunch** | 1 serving *Creamless Cream of Cauliflower Soup* (page 76)<br>Chicken salad made with leftover roasted chicken from Day 1:<br>1 serving of roasted chicken on a generous bed of mixed greens and chopped salad vegetables; 1 tablespoon olive oil mixed with balsamic vinegar to taste |

| | |
|---|---|
| **Snack** | 1 cup low-fat, sugar-free yogurt (any flavor) |

| | |
|---|---|
| **Dinner** | 1 serving *Dijon-Roasted Salmon* (page 128)<br>Broccoli, steamed or boiled<br>Carrots, cooked |

*Daily Nutrition Profile:* 1,244 calories; 91 g protein; 113 g carbohydrate; 51 g total fat; 9 g saturated fat; 383 mg cholesterol; 17 g fiber; 1 g sugar; 1,435 mg sodium

# Day 3

| | |
|---|---|
| **Breakfast** | 2 slices fat-free ham |
| | 1 serving *Forget-the-Fat Granola* (page 63) mixed with 1 cup low-fat, sugar-free yogurt (any flavor) |
| | 1 orange |
| | Coffee or tea |
| **Snack** | 1 apple, sliced and dipped in *Fruit Dip* (page 169) |
| **Lunch** | 1 serving *Three Bean Chili* (page 134) |
| | Side salad of shredded romaine lettuce with an assortment of other chopped salad vegetables, 2 tablespoons reduced-fat Caesar salad dressing |
| **Snack** | 1/2 cup low-fat cottage cheese with baby carrots and other cut-up raw vegetables |
| **Dinner** | 1 serving *Herbed Beef Tenderloin* (page 96) |
| | Green peas, boiled |
| | Cauliflower, steamed or boiled |

*Daily Nutrition Profile:* 1,274 calories; 97 g protein; 177 g carbohydrate; 27 g total fat; 7 g saturated fat; 149 mg cholesterol; 36 g fiber; 3 g sugar; 2,787 mg sodium

# Day 4

| | |
|---|---|
| **Breakfast** | 1 serving *Mushroom-Tomato Frittata* (page 54) |
| | 1 cup skim or low-fat milk |
| | Wedge of cantaloupe (or other fresh seasonal fruit) |
| | Coffee or tea |
| **Snack** | 1 cup fresh berries |
| **Lunch** | 1 serving *Tuna Salad Wrap* (page 91) |
| **Snack** | 1 cup low-fat, sugar-free yogurt (any flavor) |
| **Dinner** | 1 serving *Italian Roast Pork Loin* (page 106) |
| | Brussels sprouts, steamed or boiled |
| | Tossed salad with 2 tablespoons low-fat Italian salad dressing |

*Daily Nutrition Profile:* 1,025 calories; 87 g protein; 102 g carbohydrate; 32 g total fat; 7 g saturated fat; 363 mg cholesterol; 25 g fiber; .5 g sugar; 2,375 mg sodium

# Day 5

| | |
|---|---|
| **Breakfast** | 2 egg whites, scrambled |
| | 1 *Orange Raisin Bran Muffin* (page 68) |
| | 1 cup low-fat or skim milk |
| | 1 cup raspberries (or other fresh seasonal fruit) |
| | Coffee or tea |
| **Snack** | Assorted cut-up raw vegetables |
| | 1 ounce reduced-fat Swiss cheese |
| **Lunch** | 1 serving *Turkey Vegetable Soup* (page 125) |
| | Shredded cabbage tossed with 2 tablespoons low-fat cole slaw dressing |
| **Snack** | 1 pear, sliced and dipped in *Fruit Dip* (page 169) |
| **Dinner** | 1 serving *Moroccan Chicken* (page 120) |

*Daily Nutrition Profile:* 1,195 calories; 95 g protein; 134 g carbohydrate; 36 g total fat; 2 g saturated fat; 203 mg cholesterol; 22 g fiber; 10 g sugar; 1,752 mg sodium

# Day 6

| | |
|---|---|
| **Breakfast** | 1 serving *Succotash Omelet* (page 56)<br>1 fresh nectarine or peach<br>Coffee or tea |
| **Snack** | ½ cup low-fat, sugar-free yogurt |
| **Lunch** | Broiled hamburger patty, extra lean, about 4 ounces<br>1 serving *Radish Slaw* (page 154)<br>¾ cup grapes |
| **Snack** | ½ cup low-fat cottage cheese with cut-up raw vegetables |
| **Dinner** | 1 serving *Halibut Baked in Packets* (page 127)<br>Tossed salad with 2 tablespoons reduced-fat salad dressing<br>1 serving *Banana Cream Pie* (page 176) |

*Daily Nutrition Profile:* 1,286 calories; 100 g protein; 146 g carbohydrate; 37 g total fat; 9 g saturated fat; 341 mg cholesterol; 12 g fiber; 5 g sugar; 1,990 mg sodium

# Day 7

| | |
|---|---|
| **Breakfast** | 1 egg, scrambled |
| | Oat bran, cooked |
| | 1 cup low-fat milk |
| | Honeydew melon (or other fresh seasonal fruit) |
| | Coffee or tea |
| **Snack** | 1 apple, sliced and dipped in *Fruit Dip* (page 169) |
| **Lunch** | 1 serving *Ratatouille* (page 151) topped with ½ cup cubed tofu (for protein) |
| | Tossed salad with 2 tablespoons reduced-fat Italian dressing |
| **Snack** | 1 cup low-fat, sugar-free plain yogurt mixed with 1 tablespoon sugar-free strawberry preserves |
| **Dinner** | 1 serving *Pot Roast Southern Style* (page 98) |
| | 1 serving *Roasted Vegetables* (page 200) |

*Daily Nutrition Profile:* 1,189 calories; 94 g protein; 151 g carbohydrate; 29 g total fat; 5 g saturated fat; 322 mg cholesterol; 24 g fiber; 1 g sugar; 1,345 mg sodium

# Day 8

| | |
|---|---|
| **Breakfast** | 2 links turkey sausage |
| | 1 cup low-fat, sugar-free yogurt (any flavor) |
| | ½ grapefruit |
| | Coffee or tea |
| **Snack** | Cucumber, sliced and dipped in ½ cup low-fat cottage cheese |
| **Lunch** | 1 serving *Curried Lentil Stew* (page 138) |
| | Tossed salad, with 2 tablespoons reduced-fat salad dressing |
| **Snack** | 1 fresh pear (or other fresh seasonal fruit) |
| **Dinner** | 1 serving *No-Fry Chicken-Fried Steak* (page 104) |
| | Tomatoes, stewed |
| | Cauliflower, steamed or boiled |

*Daily Nutrition Profile:* 1,189 calories; 107 g protein; 150 g carbohydrate; 23 g total fat; 6 g saturated fat; 141 mg cholesterol; 29 g fiber; 0 g sugar; 2,776 mg sodium

# Day 9

| | |
|---|---|
| **Breakfast** | 2 slices turkey bacon<br>Smoothie: 1 cup low-fat milk blended with 1 cup fresh blueberries<br>    and 3 tablespoons old-fashioned oats<br>Coffee or tea |
| **Snack** | 1 apple, sliced and dipped in *Fruit Dip* (page 169) |
| **Lunch** | 1 serving *Mushroom-Leek Soup* (page 79)<br>Broiled hamburger patty, extra lean, about 4 ounces |
| **Snack** | ³⁄₄ cup low-fat, sugar-free yogurt (any flavor) |
| **Dinner** | 1 serving *Apricot-Glazed Chicken Breasts* (page 119)<br>Yellow snap beans, boiled<br>Fresh tomato, sliced, topped with 1 tablespoon mayonnaise<br>1 serving *Grasshopper Pie* (page 180) |

*Daily Nutrition Profile:* 1,387 calories; 98 g protein; 156 g carbohydrate; 45 g total fat; 11 g saturated fat; 205 mg cholesterol; 19 g fiber; 6 g sugar; 1,744 mg sodium

# Day 10

| | |
|---|---|
| **Breakfast** | 2 egg whites, scrambled |
| | 1 serving *Forget-the-Fat Granola* (page 63) |
| | 1 cup low-fat, skim, or soy milk |
| | 1 banana |
| | Coffee or tea |
| **Snack** | 1 fresh plum (or other fresh seasonal fruit) |
| **Lunch** | 1 serving *Mexicali Layered Salad* (page 85) |
| **Snack** | 1 cup low-fat, sugar-free yogurt (any flavor) |
| **Dinner** | 1 serving *Steamed Whole Red Snapper* (page 205) |
| | Mixed vegetables, steamed (broccoli, zucchini, yellow squash), with 1 tablespoon trans-free margarine |

*Daily Nutrition Profile:* 1,259 calories; 111 g protein; 176 g carbohydrate; 22 g total fat; 2 g saturated fat; 196 mg cholesterol; 31 g fiber; 1 g sugar; 1,880 mg sodium

# Day 11

| | |
|---|---|
| **Breakfast** | 1 egg, poached |
| | 1 *Refrigerator Applesauce Bran Muffin* (page 70) |
| | 1 orange |
| | Coffee or tea |
| **Snack** | Fruit smoothie: 1 cup of low-fat, skim, or soy milk blended with 1/2 cup berries, with artificial sweetener (optional) |
| **Lunch** | Ground turkey, lean, broiled or grilled (about 4 ounces) |
| | 1 serving *Instant Gazpacho* (page 78) |
| **Snack** | Cut-up raw chopped vegetables dipped in 1/2 cup low-fat cottage cheese |
| **Dinner** | 1 serving *Poached Cod with Warm Pineapple Salsa* (page 130) |
| | Tossed salad with 1 tablespoon olive oil and balsamic vinegar to taste |

*Daily Nutrition Profile:* 1,050 calories; 95 g protein; 106 g carbohydrate; 29 g total fat; 3 g saturated fat; 344 mg cholesterol; 23 g fiber; 6 g sugar; 1,394 mg sodium

# Day 12

| | |
|---|---|
| **Breakfast** | 1 serving *Mushroom-Tomato Frittata* (page 54) |
| | ¾ cup low-fat, skim, or soy milk |
| | 1 cup fresh raspberries |
| | Coffee or tea |
| **Snack** | 1 serving *Stuffed Dates* (page 170) |
| **Lunch** | 1 serving *Curried Tabbouleh* (with chicken, page 86) |
| | Tossed salad with 2 tablespoons reduced-fat salad dressing |
| **Snack** | Cut-up raw vegetables dipped in ½ cup low-fat cottage cheese |
| **Dinner** | 1 serving *Beef and Broccoli Stir-Fry* (page 100) |
| | 1 serving *Vanilla-and-Orange Parfait* (page 182) |

*Daily Nutrition Profile:* 1,343 calories; 99 g protein; 182 g carbohydrate; 27 g total fat; 5 g saturated fat; 324 mg cholesterol; 28 g fiber; 7 g sugar; 2,297 mg sodium

# Day 13

| | |
|---|---|
| **Breakfast** | 2 egg whites, scrambled<br>1 *Orange Raisin Bran Muffin* (page 68)<br>1 cup melon balls (or other fresh seasonal fruit)<br>Coffee or tea |
| **Snack** | 1 orange |
| **Lunch** | Low-fat chef's salad: 2 slices reduced-fat ham, 1 ounce low-fat Cheddar cheese, chopped lettuce and assorted cut-up salad vegetables, 2 tablespoons low-fat French dressing |
| **Snack** | 1 cup low-fat, sugar-free yogurt (any flavor) |
| **Dinner** | 1 serving *Dijon-Roasted Salmon* (page 128)<br>1 serving *Winter Root Vegetable Puree* (page 150) |

*Daily Nutrition Profile:* 961 calories; 71 g protein; 107 g carbohydrate; 32 g total fat; 7 g saturated fat; 119 mg cholesterol; 17 g fiber; 3 g sugar; 1,485 mg sodium

# Day 14

| | |
|---|---|
| **Breakfast** | 2 links turkey sausage |
| | 1 serving ($1/2$ cup) high-fiber cereal, such as All-Bran |
| | 1 cup low-fat, skim, or soy milk |
| | 1 peach (or other fresh seasonal fruit) |
| | Coffee or tea |
| **Snack** | $1/2$ cup low-fat, sugar-free yogurt (any flavor) |
| **Lunch** | 1 serving *Seared Tuna Salad* (page 83) |
| **Snack** | 1 serving *Curried Tofu* Dip (page 194) with raw cut-up vegetables |
| **Dinner** | 1 serving *Zucchini Lasagna* (page 144) |
| | Tossed salad with 2 tablespoons reduced-fat blue cheese dressing |
| | 1 serving *Baked Bananas* (page 187) |

*Daily Nutrition Profile:* 1,269 calories; 106 g protein; 163 g carbohydrate; 30 g total fat; 9 g saturated fat; 181 mg cholesterol; 31 g fiber; 14 g sugar; 2,463 mg sodium

# Setting Up a
# No-Fail Kitchen

It's almost impossible to overemphasize the influence your environment has on your food choices and on your ability to manage your weight successfully over the long term. In *The Ultimate Weight Solution*, key 3—a no-fail environment—deals with changing the personal landscape of your life (including your home) by eliminating anything that will set you up for failure and incorporating, as much as possible, everything that will support your weight loss goals.

The presence of food in your environment is one of the most insistent of all triggers to eat, overeat, or binge. Thus, key 3 is all about removing tempting food from your home, office, car, or anywhere you normally store it. After all, you can't eat what is not there.

One of the most important places to start applying this key is right in your own kitchen. Specifically, I would like you to take an inventory of your kitchen, looking for and tossing out all low-response cost, low-yield foods and replacing them with high-response cost, high-yield foods. Let me give you some general suggestions as to how to do this:

• Replace cookies, candy, and any high-calorie, sweetened snack foods with fruits and vegetables.

• Replace salty foods such as potato chips, pretzels, taco chips, nuts, and other packaged munchies with those of a more whole-some nature, such as whole-grain crackers or air-popped pop-corn.

• Replace sweet rolls, pastries, doughnuts, cakes, snack cakes, pies, and other baked sweets with fruits or the healthy snacks and desserts featured in this cookbook.

• Replace sugary breakfast cereals with whole-grain and high-fiber cereals.

• Replace white bread, white rolls, and white buns with their whole-grain counterparts.

• Replace high-fat cold cuts with their fat-free or reduced-fat equivalents.

• Replace ice cream and high-sugar frozen desserts with fat-free, sugar-free ice milks and frozen yogurt.

• Replace quick-fix prepared foods such as pizza, fried entrées, TV dinners, and microwaveable sandwiches with lean cuts of meat; poultry, such as chicken and turkey breasts (prepared with-out skin); fresh, frozen, or canned seafood (nothing that is breaded, however).

• Replace butter, stick margarine, and shortening with healthy fats such as olive oil or canola oil.

• Replace whole-fat dairy products with reduced-fat or fat-free skim milk, low-fat milk, sugar-free yogurt, or low-fat cheeses.

• Replace sugared soft drinks and beverages, including flavored coffees, with bottled water and other noncaloric beverages.

Ridding your kitchen of low-response cost, low-yield foods and replacing them with healthier ones is a key step toward *programming,* or setting up your world so that it supports your goals. Programming helps you get past needing to feel motivated all the time to try to lose weight. When your enthusiasm flags and your willpower conks out—which it will—you need to be in an environment that will prop you up. If you don't pull this off, the availability of binge foods and other items that can threaten to derail effective weight management will rear up to sabotage you.

Think about it: Perhaps one of the reasons you haven't met your weight loss goals in the past is that you let yourself get away with not doing what was needed when it was needed. You kept failing by degrees, falling farther and farther short of the outcome you wanted. When you redesign your environment according to the guidelines in key 3, you are programming yourself for a different outcome—success.

So, let's plan to further that momentum toward success right away by talking about what you will need to keep in stock at various times to prepare the recipes in this book and create a no-fail kitchen.

# Stocking Your Kitchen

The foods I have listed for you here are the specific ingredients called for to prepare the recipes in this book. As you plan your meals and make up your shopping list for the week, you can pick and choose the ones you'll need. Many are staples, such as canned goods, frozen foods, seasonings, and spices you will want to have on hand when you're ready to prepare a recipe.

## High-Response Cost, High-Yield Proteins

| | |
|---|---|
| **Beef and Other Meats** | Beef tenderloin |
| | Eye round of beef |
| | Top round of beef |
| | Sirloin steaks |
| | Ground beef, extra lean |
| | Ground veal, lean |
| | Lamb chops, loin |
| | Leg of lamb |
| | Pork loin |
| | Pork tenderloin |
| **Chicken and Poultry** | Chicken breasts, skinless and boneless |
| | Chicken thighs, skinless and boneless |
| | Chicken, whole, roasting |
| | Low-fat turkey sausage, including links |
| | Turkey bacon |
| | Turkey breast |

| | |
|---|---|
| **Eggs and Low-Fat Dairy Foods** | Buttermilk, low-fat or fat-free |
| | Cheddar cheese, low-fat |
| | Cottage cheese, low-fat or fat-free |
| | Cream cheese, fat-free |
| | Eggs |
| | Egg substitute |
| | Mexican cheese blend, shredded, low-fat |
| | Milk, fat-free evaporated, canned |
| | Milk, low-fat or skim |
| | Milk, nonfat dry |
| | Mozzarella cheese, low-fat |
| | Parmesan cheese, low-fat |
| | Provolone cheese, low-fat |
| | Ricotta cheese, low-fat |
| | Sour cream, fat-free |
| | Yogurt, low-fat, sugar-free versions (plain and flavored) |
| | Yogurt, fat-free, sugar-free, frozen |
| **Fish** | Cod |
| | Crabmeat, lump |
| | Halibut |
| | Red snapper |
| | Salmon |
| | Shrimp, frozen, including cocktail size |
| | Tuna, fresh |
| | Tuna, canned, solid white, water-packed |
| **Soy and Vegetarian Foods** | Soy milk |
| | Tofu, silken, light |
| | Tofu, silken, soft |

# High-Response Cost, High-Yield Carbohydrates

| | |
|---|---|
| **Fruits** | Apples |
| | Applesauce, unsweetened |
| | Apple juice, unsweetened |
| | Avocado |
| | Bananas |
| | Blackberries, fresh and frozen |
| | Cherries (unsweetened), frozen and canned |
| | Cherry pie filling, sugar-free |
| | Dates |
| | Fruit, dried, (apple rings, apricot halves, black mission figs, blueberries, cherries, cranberries, peaches, raisins, including golden) |
| | Grapefruit |
| | Grapes, red or green, seedless |
| | Lemons |
| | Limes |
| | Mandarin oranges (juice or water-packed), canned |
| | Oranges |
| | Orange juice, unsweetened |
| | Peaches (unsweetened), frozen |
| | Pears |
| | Pineapple chunks (juice or water-packed), canned |
| | Pineapple juice (unsweetened) |
| | Prunes |
| | Raspberries (unsweetened), frozen |
| | Strawberries, fresh |

**Nonstarchy Vegetables***

Artichokes, canned
Asparagus
Bean sprouts, canned
Beets
Beet greens
Bell peppers, green and red
Broccoli, frozen
Brussels sprouts
Cabbage, including napa
Carrots
Carrots, baby
Celery
Cucumbers
Cauliflower, frozen
Eggplant
Garlic cloves
Green beans
Green chiles, canned, mild or hot
Hearts of palm, canned
Jalapeños, pickled
Jicama
Leeks
Mixed greens
Mushrooms, button
Onions, red and white
Parsnips
Peas, frozen
Peas and carrots, frozen
Pimentos, in a jar or can
Radishes

* These vegetables contain varying degrees of starch, but tend to be lower in carbohydrates than the starchy vegetables listed on page 40.

Romaine lettuce

Rutabaga

Scallions

Shiitake or porcini mushrooms

Snow peas

Spaghetti squash

Spinach, baby

Swiss chard

Tomatoes, fresh, Roma and cherry

Tomatoes, canned

Tomatoes, sun-dried

Turnips

Vegetable juice

Yellow squash

Zucchini

---

**Starchy Vegetables**

Acorn squash

Black beans, canned

Black-eyed peas

Chickpeas (garbanzos), canned

Corn, frozen or canned

Frozen mixed vegetables (succotash)

Great Northern beans (white beans), canned

Lentils, green, dried

Lima beans, frozen

Pinto beans, canned

Potatoes, russet baking

Pumpkin, canned

Red kidney beans, canned

Sweet potatoes

White beans, canned

| | |
|---|---|
| **Whole Grain Products and Cereals** | Brown rice |
| | Bulgur wheat |
| | Cereals (All-Bran, Banana Nut Crunch Cereal, Grape Nuts, Great Grains with Crunchy Pecans) |
| | Chinese noodles, enriched, or Japanese somen or udon noodles |
| | Corn tortillas |
| | Grits, yellow or white |
| | Oat bran |
| | Oat flour |
| | Oatmeal, old-fashioned |
| | Quinoa |
| | Soba noodles |
| | Wheat bran |
| | Wheat germ |
| | Whole-grain bread |
| | Whole-grain crackers, such as Triscuits |
| | Whole-wheat breadcrumbs |
| | Whole-wheat elbow macaroni |
| | Whole-wheat flour |
| | Whole-wheat tortillas, fat-free |

# High-Response Cost, High-Yield Fats

| | |
|---|---|
| **Fats and Oils** | Canola oil |
| | Hazelnut oil |
| | Light margarine spread, trans free |
| | Olive oil |
| | Peanut oil |
| | Sesame oil |
| | Vegetable oil |
| | Walnut oil |

| | |
|---|---|
| **Nuts and Seeds** | Almonds |
| | Sunflower seeds |
| | Walnuts |

# High-Response Cost, High-Yield Condiments

| | |
|---|---|
| **Broths** | Chicken, fat-free, salt-free |
| | Vegetable broth, fat-free, salt-free |
| **Mustards** | Dijon mustard |
| **Sauces** | Cocktail sauce |
| | Marinara sauce |
| | Salsa |
| | Soy sauce, reduced-sodium |
| | Tabasco |
| | Teriyaki sauce |
| | Worcestershire sauce |
| **Vinegars** | Apple-cider vinegar |
| | Balsamic vinegar |
| | Rice vinegar |
| | White wine vinegar |
| **Spices and Herbs** | Allspice, ground and whole berries |
| | Apple-pie spice |
| | Barbecue dry rub |
| | Basil, dried |
| | Bay leaf |
| | Black pepper |
| | Black peppercorns, whole |
| | Cardamom pods |
| | Cayenne pepper |
| | Celery seed |
| | Chili powder |

Cilantro, fresh leaves

Cinnamon

Cinnamon sticks

Cloves, whole

Crushed red-pepper flakes

Cumin, ground and seeds

Curry powder

Dehydrated onion

Dill weed, dried and fresh

Dry mustard

Fennel seed

Five-spice powder

Garlic powder

Ginger, fresh and dried ground

Lemon pepper, no salt

Liquid smoke

Meat tenderizer

Mint, fresh leaves

Nutmeg, whole or ground

Onion powder

Oregano, dried

Paprika, mild

Parsley, fresh flat-leaf

Poppy seeds

Pumpkin-pie spice

Rosemary

Saffron threads

Sage, rubbed

Sage leaves, fresh

Tarragon, fresh and dried

Thyme, fresh and dried

Turmeric

| **Sweeteners** | All-fruit preserves, apricot |
| | Chocolate syrup, fat-free, sugar-free |
| | Granulated sugar substitute, such as Equal, Splenda, Sweet'n Low |
| | Maple syrup, sugar-free |
| | Orange marmalade, sugar-free |

| **Extracts and Flavorings** | Almond extract |
| | Maple extract |
| | Mint or peppermint extract |
| | Pure vanilla extract |
| | Rum extract |

| **Mayonnaises and Salad Dressings** | Caesar salad dressing, reduced-fat |
| | Commercial salad dressing, reduced-fat |
| | Italian salad dressing, reduced-fat |
| | Mayonnaise, fat-free |
| | Soy mayonnaise |

| **Fruit Juice Concentrates** | Apple-juice concentrate, unsweetened |
| | Orange-juice concentrate, unsweetened |
| | Pineapple-juice concentrate, unsweetened |
| | White-grape juice concentrate, unsweetened |

| **Gelatin and Pudding Mixes** | Banana pudding mix, fat-free, sugar-free |
| | Chocolate pudding mix, fat-free, sugar-free |
| | Lime Jell-O, sugar-free |
| | Orange Jell-O, sugar-free |
| | Vanilla pudding mix, fat-free, sugar-free |

**Other**

Assorted teas

Baking soda

Baking powder

Capers

Cornstarch (thickening agent)

Dill pickles

Espresso or coffee powder

Horseradish, white

Japanese dried seaweed (nori)

Lemon-lime soda, sugar-free

Seltzer, raspberry-flavored

Tahini

Tomato paste

Vegetable spray, olive oil, regular, and butter-flavored

Wasabi paste or powder

# Equipping Your Kitchen

Outfitting your kitchen with the equipment you'll need to create delicious, healthful meals is as important to you as having the proper tools is to a carpenter. With the right tools, cooking is easier, more fun, and much more nutritious. To help you, I have provided a list of equipment below. Some of these items may seem obvious and will already be in your kitchen artillery; others represent nice-to-haves but may not be essential. I am not advocating that you go out and buy every single thing on the list you don't already have. If it's a kitchen tool you may use only once in a while, consider borrowing it from a friend or neighbor rather than investing in it now. With this in mind, here is a rundown of the equipment used in these recipes, so that you will understand what it takes to cook well and shape up your health in the process.

| | |
|---|---|
| **Pots, Pans, and Special Dishes** | Casserole dish, glass |
| | Colander |
| | Custard cups |
| | Gelatin mold, 2-quart |
| | Skillets—small, medium, and large, nonstick |
| | Salad bowl |
| | Saucepans—small, medium, and large, with lids |
| | Sauté pan |
| | Stockpot |
| | Baking dishes, glass |
| | Baking pan, 8-inch square |
| | Baking sheet, large, rimmed |
| | Baking sheet, 9 x 13–inch, nonstick |
| | Broiler pan |

Dutch oven

Parfait glasses

Punch bowl

Mixing bowls—small, medium, and large

Microwaveable bowls and containers

Muffin tins

Ovenproof saucepan

Shallow roasting pan

Soufflé dish

Springform pan

Thermos, 2-cup

Pie pan, 9-inch

Wire rack

Wok, nonstick

**Appliances**

Blender

Electric mixer

Food processor

Grill, gas or charcoal

Spice grinder

**Utensils**

Box grater

Chef's knife

Citrus zester

Fine-mesh sieve

Grapefruit spoon

Instant-read thermometer

Ladle

Measuring cups and spoons

Melon baller

Paring knife

Potato masher

Rubber spatula

Salad tongs
Spoons—all sizes, including a wooden spoon
Wire whisk

---

**Other**

Aluminum foil
Wax paper
Zipper plastic bags

There you have it—everything you need to create a no-fail, health-conscious kitchen. Now it's up to you. Consider all the ways you can begin to make healthy cooking habits and nutritious food choices a more integral part of your daily life. Remember, this is the beginning of a brand new way of cooking and, more important, a better way of living.

Refrigerator Applesauce Bran Muffins, page 70, and No-Fuss Sunrise Smoothie, page 73.

Mushroom-Tomato Frittata, page 54.

Instant Gazpacho, page 78.

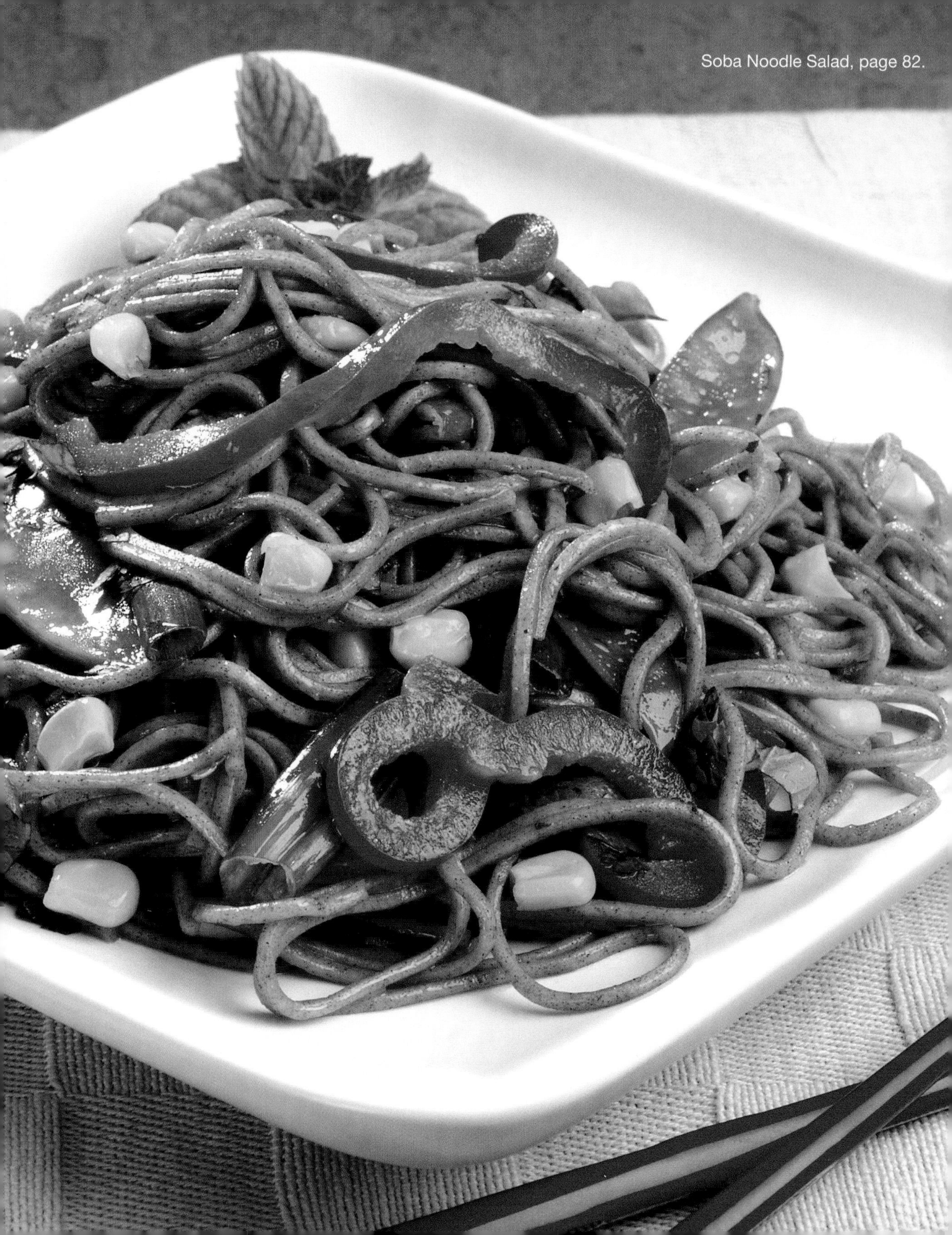
Soba Noodle Salad, page 82.

Seared Tuna Salad, page 83.

Curried Tabbouleh, page 86.

The New BLT, page 90.

Grilled Vegetable Wrap, page 92.

# The
# Recipes

# Breakfasts

There is a powerful, yet simple way to keep pounds off and guard against obesity—something that more of us should be doing to help but aren't. What is it? Eating breakfast. Research shows unequivocally that people who eat breakfast have up to 50 percent less chance than those who don't of becoming obese or developing blood sugar problems that can lead to diabetes. By properly fueling your body, breakfast has the important effect of helping you manage your hunger throughout the day, so that you do not cave in to cravings or gorge on calorie-empty food you do not need. Breakfast also keeps your metabolism well-stoked, so that your body burns calories from sunup to sundown. Further, breakfast keeps you energized, physically and mentally, for whatever stresses or demands your day might bring. Having breakfast is thus a crucial part of creating a lifestyle that supports lifelong weight control and good health.

Many of you out there are going to say, "I don't have time to fix or eat breakfast." I hear you; sometimes this is a lot easier said than done. I suspect that, if you are married with children, you are rolling out of bed early and scrambling to get your kids, yourself, and your spouse all up and out the door in some sort of reasonable and timely fashion. Let me reassure you that the recipes you will find here are designed to be cooked and served in a relatively short time; in fact, several can be prepared ahead of time and take only minutes to fix in the morning. If skipping breakfast has become an ingrained pattern and habit of behaving, then you must resolve to change. Just by implementing this simple control in your life—beginning the day with a healthy breakfast—you will have taken a positive step toward weight loss freedom.

# Mushroom-Tomato Frittata

| NUTRIENT ANALYSIS | |
|---|---|
| Calories | 106 |
| Protein | 8 g |
| Carbohydrate | 4 g |
| Total Fat | 7 g |
| Saturated Fat | 2 g |
| Cholesterol | 216 mg |
| Fiber | 1 g |
| Sugars | 0 g |
| Sodium | 100 mg |

Each serving counts as 1 protein and 1 nonstarchy vegetable.

This Spanish-inspired frittata is certainly the breakfast of champions: high in protein and nourishing vegetables. It is similar to an omelet, with the difference that, in a frittata, the vegetables are cooked right along with the eggs, whereas in an omelet they are folded into the egg as a filling. Enjoy!

**6 servings**

2 teaspoons olive oil
6 ounces button mushrooms, thinly sliced (about 3 cups)
1 medium tomato, chopped
1 teaspoon dried thyme
1 teaspoon salt
$1/2$ teaspoon dried rosemary, crumbled
$1/2$ teaspoon freshly ground black pepper
$1^1/2$ cups pasteurized egg substitute, or 6 large eggs,
    beaten until foamy
2 tablespoons grated low-fat Parmesan cheese ($1/2$ ounce)

1. Heat the oil in a 10-inch nonstick skillet set over medium heat. Add the mushrooms and cook, stirring occasionally, until they give off their liquid, liquid comes to a simmer, then reduces to a glaze, about 4 minutes.

2. Stir in the tomato, thyme, salt, rosemary, and pepper; cook 20 seconds, until aromatic. Pour in the pasteurized egg substitute or eggs, making sure the vegetables are evenly distributed, and sprinkle the Parmesan over the top. Cover, reduce the heat to low, and cook until set, about 12 minutes. Cut into six wedges and serve.

**NOTE:** If desired, you can brown the top of the frittata. Preheat the broiler while the frittata is cooking. Once set, place it about 5 inches from the heat source for about 20 seconds, just until the top is lightly browned. (Make sure your skillet's handle can withstand direct heat. If not, wrap it tightly in aluminum foil before placing it under the broiler.)

# Succotash Omelet

**NUTRIENT ANALYSIS**

| | |
|---|---|
| Calories | 173 |
| Protein | 9 g |
| Carbohydrate | 13 g |
| Total Fat | 9.5 g |
| Saturated Fat | 2 g |
| Cholesterol | 215 mg |
| Fiber | 3 g |
| Sugars | 0 g |
| Sodium | 109 mg |

Each serving counts as 1 protein, ¹⁄₂ starchy carbohydrate, and 1 nonstarchy vegetable.

When it comes to the most important meal of the day, some foods are decidedly better than others, and one of my favorites is this delicious omelet made with high-fiber lima beans, corn, and other vegetables. It provides a balanced mix of nutrients that support brain function: lean protein, quality carbohydrates, and various B vitamins. Nutrition aside, this omelet just tastes really, really good.

**4 servings**

1 tablespoon canola oil
1 small onion, chopped, or ¹⁄₃ cup frozen chopped onion
1 red bell pepper, cored, seeded, and chopped
¹⁄₂ cup frozen lima beans, thawed (*see* Note)
¹⁄₂ cup frozen corn, thawed
¹⁄₂ teaspoon dried thyme
¹⁄₂ teaspoon salt
¹⁄₄ teaspoon freshly ground black pepper
¹⁄₈ teaspoon cayenne pepper, optional
1 cup pasteurized egg substitute, or 4 large eggs, beaten until foamy
2 tablespoons shredded low-fat cheese, such as low-fat mozzarella or Cheddar (¹⁄₂ ounce)

1. Heat 2 teaspoons of the oil in a 10-inch nonstick skillet set over medium heat. Add the onion and bell pepper and cook, stirring, until softened, about 2 minutes. Add the lima beans and corn or the mixed vegetable medley, and the thyme, salt, pepper, and cayenne, if using. Cook, stirring, until warmed through, about 1 minute. Transfer the mixture to a bowl and set aside.

2. Return the skillet to medium heat. Add the remaining teaspoon of canola oil and pour in the egg substitute or the eggs. Cook without stirring until the edges begin to set, about 30 seconds. With a rubber spatula or a wooden spoon, push the cooked edges toward the center and tilt the pan so that the uncooked eggs run to the edges. Repeat this process once more, then sprinkle the cheese over the top. Cook until top is set, about 1 more minute. Spoon the succotash filling over half the omelet and gently fold the other half over the vegetables to cover them. Tilting the pan, so that the omelet rolls closed like a burrito or a crepe, carefully slide it out onto a cutting board or serving plate. Slice into 4 wedges and serve immediately.

**NOTE:** You can substitute 1 cup frozen mixed vegetables (a mixture that includes lima beans and corn), thawed, for the frozen lima beans and corn.

# Tex-Mex Scramble

**NUTRIENT ANALYSIS**

| | |
|---|---|
| Calories | 190 |
| Protein | 17 g |
| Carbohydrate | 3 g |
| Total Fat | 12 g |
| Saturated Fat | 5 g |
| Cholesterol | 251 mg |
| Fiber | .5 g |
| Sugars | 0 g |
| Sodium | 552 mg |

Each serving counts as 1 protein and 1 nonstarchy vegetable.

If you find yourself growing weary of plain scrambled eggs, it might be time to try something new. This rendition of scrambled eggs is packed with lean proteins and spiced up with chiles, which are considered the heart and soul of Tex-Mex cooking.

**4 servings**

2 teaspoons canola oil
1 small onion, chopped, or $^1/_3$ cup frozen chopped onion
8 ready-to-eat low-fat turkey breakfast sausage links, cut into
    $^1/_2$-inch pieces
$^1/_4$ cup canned chopped green chilies, mild or hot
1 teaspoon chili powder
$^1/_2$ teaspoon ground cumin
$^1/_2$ teaspoon dried oregano
$^1/_4$ teaspoon ground cinnamon
$^1/_4$ teaspoon salt
1 cup pasteurized egg substitute, or 4 large eggs, beaten
    until foamy

1. Heat the oil in a large nonstick skillet set over medium heat. Add the onion and cook, stirring, until softened, about 2 minutes. Add the sausage and cook, stirring, until lightly browned, about 2 minutes. If grease has pooled in the pan, drain it, retaining the onion and sausage.

2. Add the chilies, chili powder, cumin, oregano, cinnamon, and salt, and cook until fragrant, about 20 minutes. Pour in the pasteurized egg substitute or eggs and cook, stirring, just until scrambled (when eggs are no longer runny), a little less than 1 minute. Serve at once.

# The New *Huevos Rancheros*

A popular Tex-Mex breakfast specialty, *huevos rancheros* (eggs ranch-style), is comprised of cooked eggs on a tortilla smothered in salsa. There are more high-response cost, high-yield foods packed into a single serving than you will find in most breakfast dishes.

**6 servings**

2 medium tomatoes, quartered
2 tablespoons packed fresh cilantro leaves (*see* Note 1)
2 tablespoons chopped red onion
$1/2$ teaspoon salt
2–4 dashes Tabasco sauce
$1/4$ cup canned black beans, drained and rinsed
1 tablespoon apple-cider vinegar (*see* Note 2)
6 large eggs
6 fat-free whole-wheat tortillas
6 tablespoons low-fat shredded cheese, such as a Mexican
    cheese blend

1. Place the tomatoes and cilantro in a food processor fitted with the chopping blade and pulse three or four times, until finely chopped. Add the onion, salt, and Tabasco and pulse two or three more times, until the mixture looks like a chunky salsa. Transfer to a medium bowl, stir in the black beans, and set aside.

2. Fill a large high-sided skillet or sauté pan with water to a depth of 1 inch. Add the vinegar and bring to a boil over high heat. Reduce heat to medium-low, break an egg into a small custard cup or tea cup, then slip the egg into boiling water. Repeat

*(continued on next page)*

The New *Huevos Rancheros (cont.)*

with the remaining eggs. Cook until the whites are firm, about 1½ minutes.

3. Meanwhile, lay the tortillas flat on six plates and top each one with ¼ cup of the salsa. Transfer the poached eggs from the pan to the plates, using a slotted spoon so they can drain and taking care not to break the yolks (*see* Note 3). Top each serving with 1 tablespoon of the shredded cheese. Serve at once.

**NOTE 1:** Fresh cilantro (also known as coriander) can be sandy. To remove the grit, fill your sink or a large bowl with cool water. Separate the cilantro leaves from the stems and discard the stems. Add the cilantro leaves to the water, stir gently, then let them stand in the water for 5 minutes. Gently remove them from the water so as not to disturb the sand that has floated to the bottom (do not drain) and wrap the leaves loosely in paper towels to dry.

**NOTE 2:** The acidic vinegar will help hold the eggs together in the boiling water as they poach.

**NOTE 3:** If desired, you can transfer the poached eggs to a plate lined with paper towels and trim the ragged ends of the whites. While unnecessary, this makes for a prettier dish. Gently transfer the trimmed eggs to the prepared plates and continue with the recipe.

# Fruit Salad with Poppy Seed Dressing

**NUTRIENT ANALYSIS**

| | |
|---|---|
| Calories | 142 |
| Protein | 5 g |
| Carbohydrate | 30 g |
| Total Fat | 1 g |
| Saturated Fat | trace |
| Cholesterol | 0 mg |
| Fiber | 4 g |
| Sugars | 2 g |
| Sodium | 36 mg |

Each serving counts as 1 fruit and ⅛ low-fat dairy product.

Yogurt is one of many dairy foods that supply calcium, a mineral that has turned out to be a bona fide fat burner. Calcium triggers the body to burn more fat and curtail the amount of new fat your body makes. Most major nutritional organizations recommend two to three servings of low-fat dairy products a day. *The Ultimate Weight Solution* food plans advise two servings per day for stage 1 and stage 2, and up to 3 servings on stage 3 for weight maintenance. This fruit salad, made with yogurt, will help put more calcium on the menu.

**4 servings**

1 cup fat-free sugar-free lemon yogurt
1 teaspoon vanilla extract
1 teaspoon poppy seeds
1 cup red or green seedless grapes
1 sweet, firm apple, such as Gala, Fuji, or Red Delicious, cored and cut into bite-sized chunks
1 large orange, peeled, white pith removed, segments cut in half
1 ripe banana, peeled and cut into ¾-inch slices
¼ cup wheat germ or Forget-the-Fat Granola (page 63)

1. Combine the yogurt, vanilla, and poppy seeds in a small bowl until well-blended.

2. Combine the grapes, apple chunks, orange sections, and banana slices in a large bowl. Add the yogurt mixture and stir to coat all the fruit. Serve at once, sprinkling 1 tablespoon of wheat germ or granola over each portion—or store, covered, in the refrigerator for up to 2 days, stirring well before topping and serving.

# Cottage Cheese Parfaits

**NUTRIENT ANALYSIS**

| | |
|---|---|
| Calories | 125 |
| Protein | 15 g |
| Carbohydrate | 18 g |
| Total Fat | trace |
| Saturated Fat | 0 g |
| Cholesterol | 0 mg |
| Fiber | 1 g |
| Sugars | 4 g |
| Sodium | 425 mg |

Each serving counts as 1 fruit and 1 low-fat dairy product.

To help you through the rush of getting up and going in the morning, I promised you breakfast recipes that could be prepared quickly, without sacrificing healthy nutrition. Here is one of the easiest and fastest of our breakfast recipes, which includes some light, quick-prep fruits for a deliciously substantial way to start your day.

**4 servings**

1 cup unsweetened applesauce
2 cups fat-free cottage cheese
1 (11-ounce) can mandarin orange slices packed in juice,
    drained (about 1¼ cups orange slices)
¼ teaspoon freshly grated or ground nutmeg
    (*see* Note, page 129)

Layer ¼ of each of the first 3 ingredients in the listed order in a parfait glass. Repeat with 3 additional glasses. Top each parfait with a pinch of nutmeg.

# Forget-the-Fat Granola

| NUTRIENT ANALYSIS | |
|---|---|
| Calories | 196 |
| Protein | 7 g |
| Carbohydrate | 35 g |
| Total Fat | 5 g |
| Saturated Fat | .5 g |
| Cholesterol | 0 mg |
| Fiber | 4.5 g |
| Sugars | trace |
| Sodium | 126 mg |

Each serving counts as 1 starchy carbohydrate.

So much of the commercially prepared granola in the supermarket is loaded with fat and a hefty amount of added sugar. One way to cut down on white sugar is to sweeten recipes with fruit juice concentrate (unsweetened, of course). If you love granola but not its overload of fat and sugar, you will love this slenderized version, naturally sweetened with apple-juice concentrate.

## 12 servings

3 cups uncooked old-fashioned rolled oats (*not* quick-cooking)
3/4 cup wheat germ
1/3 cup whole raw almonds, roughly chopped (*see* Note)
2 tablespoons shelled raw sunflower seeds
1 teaspoon ground cinnamon
1 teaspoon salt
1 cup unsweetened apple-juice concentrate, thawed
1 cup dried cranberries or raisins

1. Preheat oven to 325°F.

2. Combine the oats, wheat germ, almonds, sunflower seeds, cinnamon, and salt in a large bowl. Add the juice concentrate, stir well, and spread the mixture evenly on a large rimmed baking sheet.

3. Bake, stirring every 5 minutes or so, until lightly browned, about 40 minutes. Place baking sheet on a wire rack and cool to room temperature. Mix in the dried cranberries or raisins, then pour into a sealable container or plastic bag and store at room temperature for up to 2 months. (A serving is 1/2 cup.)

*(continued on next page)*

Forget-the-Fat Granola *(cont.)*

**NOTE:** Do not use toasted almonds or sunflower seeds in this recipe, as they will burn in the oven. Avoid packaged varieties that include salt or seasonings. Plain raw nuts and seeds are available at most gourmet markets, usually in the bulk section, and in almost all health food stores.

# Oatmeal with Dried Fruit

An excellent way to help control your hunger longer is to start your day with a hearty bowl of oatmeal, enhanced with dried fruits and the 8 grams of fiber this combination supplies. My older son, Jay, introduced our family to dried cherries, which are a sensational snack alternative to candy. Add them to oatmeal for their natural sweetness as well as for the nutrients they furnish.

**4 servings**

4 cups fat-free milk
6 dried apricot halves, preferably the tart California
    variety, chopped
¼ cup golden raisins
¼ cup dried cherries or blueberries
3 cups uncooked old-fashioned rolled oats (*not* quick-cooking)
½ teaspoon ground cinnamon
½ teaspoon almond extract
¼ teaspoon salt

| NUTRIENT ANALYSIS | |
| --- | --- |
| Calories | 369 |
| Protein | 19 g |
| Carbohydrate | 65 g |
| Total Fat | 4 g |
| Saturated Fat | 1 g |
| Cholesterol | 5 mg |
| Fiber | 8 g |
| Sugars | 7 g |
| Sodium | 221 mg |

Each serving counts as 1 starchy carbohydrate, 1 fruit, and 1 low-fat dairy product.

1. Bring the milk to a gentle simmer in a large saucepan set over medium-high heat. Stir in the apricots, raisins, and cherries or blueberries. Stir in the oats. Reduce heat to low and cook, stirring often, 2 minutes.

2. Stir in the cinnamon, almond extract, and salt, and cook, stirring, until creamy, adjusting the heat so the liquid simmers very slowly, about 3 more minutes. Let stand off the heat 3 minutes before serving.

**NOTE:** You can make this dish in the microwave. Simply place all the ingredients in a large bowl, stir well, and microwave on high for 2 minutes. Stir again, then continue heating in 1-minute increments, stirring after each, until the oatmeal is creamy, about 2 more minutes. Let stand 3 minutes before serving.

# Apple-Spiced Oat Bran

**NUTRIENT ANALYSIS**

| | |
|---|---|
| Calories | 112 |
| Protein | 4 g |
| Carbohydrate | 23 g |
| Total Fat | 2 g |
| Saturated Fat | trace |
| Cholesterol | 0 mg |
| Fiber | 4 g |
| Sugars | 0 g |
| Sodium | 15 mg |

Each serving counts as 1 starchy carbohydrate and ½ fruit.

Oat bran is a generous source of soluble fiber, known to be effective for lowering harmful cholesterol when eaten in conjunction with a low-fat diet. Here, oat bran teams with dried apples, which also contain a lot of fiber, for a nourishing, heart-healthy breakfast.

**4 servings**

3 cups water
1 cup oat bran
10 dried unsweetened unsulphured apple rings, finely chopped
1 teaspoon apple-pie spice

Place all the ingredients in a large bowl and stir well. Microwave on high for 2 minutes, then stir. Microwave in 1-minute increments, stirring after each, just until the water has been absorbed, about 2 more minutes. Let stand 5 minutes before serving.

# Chili Cheddar Grits

Cheese grits are practically a breakfast staple in our household; this recipe cuts the fat considerably by using low-fat or fat-free cheese in the recipe. The spices give these grits an unexpected kick.

**4 servings**

$2^1/4$ cups water, plus more as necessary
$^1/2$ cup quick-cooking yellow or white grits
$^1/2$ cup low-fat or fat-free shredded Cheddar cheese (2 ounces)
$^1/4$ cup canned chopped green chiles, mild or hot
$^1/2$ teaspoon ground cumin
$^1/2$ teaspoon dried oregano
$^1/2$ teaspoon salt
$^1/4$ teaspoon garlic powder

1. Bring water to a boil in a large saucepan, preferably nonstick, set over high heat, and stir in the grits. Cover and reduce heat to low. Simmer, stirring frequently, until water has been absorbed, about 5 minutes.

2. Stir in the cheese, chiles, cumin, oregano, salt, and garlic powder and cook, stirring constantly, until well-blended and bubbling, about 2 minutes. If the grits become too thick and stick to the pan, add more water, 2 tablespoons at a time, to thin them out. Let stand off the heat 3 minutes before serving.

# Orange Raisin Bran Muffins

**NUTRIENT ANALYSIS**

| | |
|---|---|
| Calories | 102 |
| Protein | 3 g |
| Carbohydrate | 17 g |
| Total Fat | 3 g |
| Saturated Fat | trace |
| Cholesterol | 18 mg |
| Fiber | 3 g |
| Sugars | 3 g |
| Sodium | 131 mg |

Each serving counts as 1 starchy carbohydrate.

Perfect for a Sunday breakfast and convenient as a grab-and-go treat on weekday mornings, these muffins provide the type of high-response cost, high-yield carbohydrates we should all be eating more of: hearty whole-wheat flour, high-fiber bran cereal, and natural juice sweeteners.

**12 muffins**

12 paper muffin-cup liners
3/4 cup fat-free milk
1/2 cup unsweetened frozen orange-juice concentrate, thawed
2 tablespoons canola oil
1 teaspoon vanilla extract
1 large egg, lightly beaten, or 1/4 cup pasteurized egg substitute
2 cups Raisin Bran cereal
1 cup whole-wheat flour
Granulated sugar substitute equal to 2 tablespoons sugar
    (see package label)
1 tablespoon baking powder
1 teaspoon ground cinnamon
1/2 teaspoon salt

1. Position a rack in the center of the oven and preheat oven to 400°F. Line a 12-cup muffin tin with the paper liners.

2. Whisk the milk, orange-juice concentrate, oil, vanilla, and egg or egg substitute in a medium bowl until uniform and set aside.

3. Mix the Raisin Bran, whole-wheat flour, sugar substitute, baking powder, cinnamon, and salt in a second bowl until uniform.

4. Pour the milk mixture into the dry ingredients and stir just until dry ingredients are moistened (some small lumps are fine). Spoon enough batter into each muffin cup to fill it ⅔ full. (Reserve any remaining batter for a second baking, if desired.)

5. Bake until golden brown, about 18 to 20 minutes. A toothpick inserted into the center of one muffin should come out clean. Cool the muffins in the tin for 3 minutes, then serve immediately or transfer the muffins to a wire rack to cool completely. Store in an airtight container at room temperature for up to 3 days.

# Refrigerator Applesauce Bran Muffins

| NUTRIENT ANALYSIS | |
|---|---|
| Calories | 108 |
| Protein | 4 g |
| Carbohydrate | 17 g |
| Total Fat | 3 g |
| Saturated Fat | .5 g |
| Cholesterol | 1 mg |
| Fiber | 4 g |
| Sugars | 1 g |
| Sodium | 98 mg |

Each serving counts as 1 starchy carbohydrate.

I can't emphasize enough how important it is to get more fiber in your diet, and these exceptionally great-tasting muffins are one way to do it. You can make this nutritionally rich batter ahead of time and store it in your refrigerator for up to three weeks, so it's ready whenever you want to bake a batch of fresh muffins for breakfast. The noncaloric sweetener transforms these muffins into wholesome sugar-free treats so you can feel good about enjoying them.

**24 muffins**

1½ cups original All-Bran cereal
1 cup oat bran
¾ cup wheat bran
½ cup uncooked old-fashioned rolled oats (*not* quick-cooking)
2½ cups boiling water
2 cups whole-wheat flour
Granulated sugar substitute equal to ½ cup sugar
   (see package label)
2 tablespoons baking soda
1 teaspoon ground cinnamon
1 teaspoon salt
2 cups low-fat or fat-free buttermilk
¾ cup unsweetened applesauce
½ cup pasteurized egg substitute
¼ cup canola oil
Paper muffin cup liners, as needed

1. Combine the All-Bran, oat bran, wheat bran, and rolled oats in a large bowl. Pour in the boiling water and stir until thoroughly moistened. Set aside for 15 minutes.

2. Meanwhile, combine the whole-wheat flour, sugar substitute, baking soda, cinnamon, and salt in a second large bowl.

3. Mash out any lumps in the bran mixture, then stir in the buttermilk, applesauce, egg substitute, and oil until smooth. Stir in the whole-wheat flour mixture until well-blended. The batter will be thick, so using an electric mixer or a potato masher might make this easier. Cover and refrigerate for up to 3 weeks.

4. To bake the muffins, position a rack in the center of the oven and preheat oven to 375°F. Line as many muffin cups as you want with paper liners and spoon batter into the prepared muffin cups until each is about ⅔ full (*see* Note).

5. Bake until puffed and golden brown, about 25 to 30 minutes. A toothpick inserted into one muffin should come out clean. Cool muffins in tin for 3 minutes, then serve at once or transfer to a wire rack to cool completely. Baked muffins can be stored in an airtight container at room temperature for up to 3 days.

**NOTE:** If you're baking less than a whole tin of muffins, fill the unused indentions halfway with water—this will keep the heat even and prevent the tin from warping.

# Peach Melba Smoothie

## NUTRIENT ANALYSIS

| | |
|---|---|
| Calories | 103 |
| Protein | 4 g |
| Carbohydrate | 20 g |
| Total Fat | 1 g |
| Saturated Fat | .5 |
| Cholesterol | 2 mg |
| Fiber | 3 g |
| Sugars | 3 g |
| Sodium | 33 mg |

Each serving counts as 1 fruit
and 1/4 low-fat dairy product.

For breakfast on the run or even for one of your between-meal snacks, there are few things more filling or satisfying than a fruit smoothie. This one supplies three types of fruit so that your body gets a host of the vitamins, minerals, antioxidants, and healthy carbohydrates critical to maintaining health and high energy levels.

## 2 servings

1/2 cup frozen sliced peaches
1/2 cup frozen raspberries
1/2 cup fat-free sugar-free vanilla yogurt
1 tablespoon wheat germ
Granulated sugar substitute equal to 1 teaspoon sugar, optional
    (see package label)
1 cup ice (*see* Note)
1/4 cup unsweetened orange-juice concentrate, thawed

Place the ingredients in the order listed in a large blender. Pulse once or twice, then blend until smooth.

**NOTE:** For best results, let the ice melt slightly, usually for about 5 minutes at room temperature. If possible, use smaller cubes—not crushed or chipped, but not the standard boxy cubes, either. If you're using standard trays, try filling them with cold (rather than hot) water before freezing—the resulting cubes will be more prone to shattering.

# No-Fuss Sunrise Smoothie

**NUTRIENT ANALYSIS**

| | |
|---|---:|
| Calories | 98 |
| Protein | 1 g |
| Carbohydrate | 24 g |
| Total Fat | 1 g |
| Saturated Fat | 0 g |
| Cholesterol | 0 mg |
| Fiber | 6 g |
| Sugars | trace |
| Sodium | 2 mg |

Each serving counts as 1 fruit.

With its mix of fruits, this smoothie is a great way to prepare healthy food fast, and it's packed with a laundry list of nutrients, including vitamin C, potassium, and fiber.

**8 servings of fruit mixture to make 8 smoothies**

Frozen fruit mixture
2 cups blackberries, fresh or frozen
2 cups raspberries, fresh or frozen
2 cups sliced fresh strawberries
2 large ripe bananas, thinly sliced

Individual smoothies
1 cup unsweetened apple juice
1/4 teaspoon vanilla extract

1. Combine the blackberries, raspberries, strawberries, and bananas in a large, resealable plastic bag and freeze overnight. The fruit will keep in the freezer for up to 4 months.

2. To make one smoothie, scoop 1 cup of the fruit mixture into a blender. Add the apple juice and vanilla and blend until smooth.

# Lunches

**4**

There is a powerful sense of well-being that comes from good nutrition, exercise, and proper weight management. Yet, sometimes, we compromise our health by grabbing food on the run without giving much conscious thought to our food choices or what they are doing to our waistlines. Creating a new, health-producing lifestyle means making thoughtful, conscious choices at every single meal. Lunch, for example, should be a healthy opportunity to refuel yourself in order to get through the rest of your day productively, so you will want to choose foods that help you to accomplish that.

Accordingly, the lunch selections in this chapter, including soups, salads, and sandwiches, provide the nutritional value and content to nourish and revitalize you. Most soups, in addition to being nutritious and healthy, support weight loss and control, and are, therefore, among the best high-response cost, high-yield foods you can include in any meal. The spectacular salads you will find here can not only make a huge impact on your vitamin profile but also furnish the fruits and vegetables that can help fight disease. And, if you've been trapped in a burgers-and-fries rut, the sandwiches will be your rescue.

So, starting today, take a fresh look at how you are nourishing yourself at midday, and shift your standards. Eating well will make you feel good about your body so that you will be naturally motivated to want to take care of it.

# Creamless Cream of Cauliflower Soup

NUTRIENT ANALYSIS

| | |
|---|---|
| Calories | 78 |
| Protein | 3 g |
| Carbohydrate | 15 g |
| Total Fat | 2 g |
| Saturated Fat | 0 g |
| Cholesterol | 0 mg |
| Fiber | 2 g |
| Sugars | 0 g |
| Sodium | 101 mg |

Each serving counts as
1 nonstarchy vegetable.
(The potato is used to thicken
the soup and is a negligible
source of starch in this recipe.)

Eating high-response cost, high-yield soups helps you feel satisfied and makes it easier to get the nutrients you require while, at the same time, consuming fewer calories. If you are having trouble controlling your urge to splurge at meals, a light soup like this one will improve your chances of losing weight. To prevent the soup from turning brown when you puree it, be sure not to brown the vegetables.

**6 servings**

2 teaspoons canola oil
1 medium onion, chopped, or ³/₄ cup frozen chopped onion
2 ribs celery, chopped
1 small head cauliflower, cut into florets, or 4 cups frozen
    cauliflower florets, thawed
1 medium baking potato (about 12 ounces), peeled and diced
1 teaspoon rubbed sage
1 teaspoon dried thyme
1 teaspoon dry mustard
1 teaspoon celery seed
4 cups no-salt, fat-free vegetable broth
¹/₂ teaspoon salt
¹/₄ teaspoon freshly ground black pepper
3 tablespoons golden raisins, for garnish

1. Heat the oil in a large saucepan set over low heat. Add the onion and celery and cook, stirring often, until golden, about 5 minutes. If the onion begins to brown, lower heat.

2. Add the cauliflower and diced potato and cook, stirring, 1 minute. Sprinkle the sage, thyme, mustard, and celery seed over the vegetables, stir well, and cook until fragrant, about 20 seconds.

3. Pour in broth and bring to a simmer. Cover, reduce heat to low, and simmer until the potato and cauliflower are soft when pierced with a fork, about 15 minutes.

4. Working in batches if necessary, puree the soup in a food processor fitted with the chopping blade or in a large blender, scraping down the sides of the bowl as necessary. Return the puree to the saucepan, again set over medium heat, and cook just until heated through, about 1 minute. Season with salt and pepper, ladle into bowls, and top each serving with $1/2$ tablespoon golden raisins.

# Instant Gazpacho

| NUTRIENT ANALYSIS | |
|---|---|
| Calories | 54 |
| Protein | 2 g |
| Carbohydrate | 11 g |
| Total Fat | trace |
| Saturated Fat | 0 g |
| Cholesterol | 0 |
| Fiber | 2 g |
| Sugars | 5 g |
| Sodium | 399 mg |

Each serving counts as
1 nonstarchy vegetable.

The food plans you follow on *The Ultimate Weight Solution* do not place limits on the amounts of nonstarchy vegetables you can eat. These vegetables are the most nutrient-packed, low-calorie foods you can include in your diet. The more vegetables you consume, the less room—or desire—you will have for low-response cost, low-yield foods. This delicious cold soup is an easy and delicious way to eat more vegetables. It can be made ahead, and it tastes even better the second day.

**10 servings**

6 cups V-8 juice
¼ cup freshly squeezed lemon juice
1 medium red onion, finely chopped
3 ribs celery, minced
2 garlic cloves, minced
1 green bell pepper, cored, seeded, and finely chopped
1 large cucumber, peeled and finely chopped (*see* Note)
1 tablespoon Worcestershire sauce
2 teaspoons salt
½ teaspoon freshly ground black pepper
3–5 dashes Tabasco sauce

Place all the ingredients in a large bowl; stir well. Cover and refrigerate at least 2 hours, or preferably overnight. The gazpacho will keep in the refrigerator, tightly covered, for 5 days.

**NOTE:** If desired, seed the cucumber before chopping it. After peeling, cut it in half the long way, forming two long canoes. Use a teaspoon or a grapefruit spoon to scrape out seeds and inner membranes.

# Mushroom-Leek Soup

**NUTRIENT ANALYSIS**

| | |
|---|---|
| Calories | 85 |
| Protein | 3 g |
| Carbohydrate | 15 g |
| Total Fat | 2.5 g |
| Saturated Fat | trace |
| Cholesterol | 0 mg |
| Fiber | 2 g |
| Sugars | 0 g |
| Sodium | 228 mg |

Each serving counts as
1 nonstarchy vegetable.

In the complex, jam-packed lives we create with kids, jobs, family, volunteer activities, and other demands on our time, there is often precious little time left over to think about mapping out nutritious meals every day of the week. Quick, easy-to-prepare soups like this one help to solve that problem. It is make-it-yourself fast food—one that is simple, low in fat, and highly nutritious. The vegetables that form its base are high in phyto-nutrients, which bring to the table an array of health-protective benefits.

**6 servings**

2 teaspoons olive oil
3 large leeks, thinly sliced (*see* Note 1)
8 ounces button mushrooms, brushed of dirt and thinly sliced
    (about 5 cups sliced mushrooms)
3 medium tomatoes, chopped (*see* Note 2)
2 teaspoons dried tarragon
1¼ teaspoons dry mustard
3 cups no-salt, fat-free vegetable broth
¾ teaspoon salt
½ teaspoon freshly ground black pepper

1. Heat the oil in a large saucepan set over medium heat. Add the leeks and cook, stirring, until softened, about 2 minutes. Add the mushrooms and tomatoes and cook, stirring often, until the mushrooms give off their liquid, and it comes to a simmer, about 3 minutes.

*(continued on next page)*

Mushroom-Leek Soup *(cont.)*

2. Stir in the tarragon and dry mustard, then pour in the broth and return mixture to a simmer. Cover, reduce heat to low, and simmer 15 minutes. Season with salt and pepper; serve at once.

**NOTE 1:** Leeks are notoriously sandy. To remove the grit, slice them in half lengthwise, leaving the inner root end intact so that the leek does not fall apart. Gently pry apart the inner rings under cold, running water, washing out any grit without causing the rings to come apart. Slice off the root end, then thinly slice the leek halves into rings, slicing apart the white sections and the first part of the pale green sections. Discard the tough, dark-green, upper leaves.

**NOTE 2:** Simply for aesthetics, some cooks prefer to seed the tomatoes so they don't see tomato seeds floating in the finished soup. To do so, slice the tomatoes into quarters, then scoop out and discard the pulpy seeds, using your thumb or fingers. Chop the seeded sections of the tomato as directed.

# Thermos Soup

| NUTRIENT ANALYSIS | |
| --- | --- |
| Calories | 159 |
| Protein | 9 g |
| Carbohydrate | 31 g |
| Total Fat | 3 g |
| Saturated Fat | 0 g |
| Cholesterol | 0 mg |
| Fiber | 8 g |
| Sugars | 0 g |
| Sodium | 318 mg |

Each serving counts as
1 nonstarchy vegetable and
1/2 starchy vegetable.

If you habitually purchase low-response cost, low-yield snacks or food from the vending machine where you work, it's time to re-evaluate what you are doing and make some changes. What I would recommend is that you start packing your own take-along lunch in order to weaken and eliminate your vending machine habit. Start with this quick, nutritious soup. Simply place the ingredients in your thermos and you will have a hunger-suppressing soup by noon. The trick is to make sure the carrot and celery are finely minced into $1/8$-inch cubes, if possible.

**1 serving**

$1^1/_2$ cups no-salt, fat-free vegetable broth
$1/_4$ cup packed baby spinach leaves (about 20 small leaves)
$1/_4$ cup frozen corn, thawed
1 small carrot, minced
1 small celery rib, minced
1 teaspoon dehydrated minced onion

1. Bring the broth to a simmer in a small saucepan set over high heat. Alternatively, bring it to a boil in a microwave-safe container, microwaving on high about 3 minutes.

2. Place the spinach, corn, carrot, celery, and minced onion in a 2-cup thermos. Pour in the broth and close tightly. Let stand at least 3 hours, or up to 5 hours, to form a rich soup.

# Soba Noodle Salad

**NUTRIENT ANALYSIS**

| | |
|---|---|
| Calories | 128 |
| Protein | 5.5 g |
| Carbohydrate | 22 g |
| Total Fat | 3 g |
| Saturated Fat | .5 g |
| Cholesterol | 0 mg |
| Fiber | 2.5 g |
| Sugars | 1 g |
| Sodium | 310 mg |

Each serving counts as approximately 1⅓ starchy carbohydrates.

Soba noodles are traditional Japanese noodles made with fiber-rich buckwheat flour. They are available in the Asian section of many supermarkets and in almost all gourmet shops. This Asian-inspired salad is easy to put together and well-suited for any event, from a party to a picnic.

**6 servings**

¼ cup rice vinegar or white wine vinegar
3 tablespoons reduced-sodium soy sauce
1 tablespoon toasted sesame oil
3 cups cooked soba noodles
1 large red or green bell pepper, cored, seeded, and thinly sliced
1 cup frozen corn, thawed
¾ cup fresh snow peas, or ¾ cup frozen snow peas, thawed
5 medium scallions, green part only, sliced into 1-inch sections
¼ cup packed fresh cilantro leaves, chopped
2 tablespoons packed fresh mint leaves, chopped

1. Whisk the vinegar, soy sauce, and sesame oil in a small bowl and set aside.

2. Toss the noodles, pepper, corn, snow peas, scallions, cilantro, and mint in a large bowl. Pour in the vinegar dressing (if it has separated, whisk again before adding), toss well, and serve at once, or cover and chill in the refrigerator up to 24 hours.

# Seared Tuna Salad

**NUTRIENT ANALYSIS**

| | |
|---|---|
| Calories | 218 |
| Protein | 36 g |
| Carbohydrate | 6 g |
| Total Fat | 5 g |
| Saturated Fat | 1 g |
| Cholesterol | 66 mg |
| Fiber | 2 g |
| Sugars | trace |
| Sodium | 191 mg |

Each serving counts as 1 protein and 1 nonstarchy vegetable.

A healthy game plan for increasing your intake of heart-healthy omega-3 fats is to find more ways to cook with tuna. With practically no effort at all, you can prepare this gourmet-inspired tuna salad and get nutrition and flavor at the same time. When purchasing tuna, check for freshness by asking to smell it. Tuna should smell fresh, like the ocean on a spring day. In this recipe, the fish is best prepared rare or medium rare, when the tuna is pink inside but crispy outside.

**4 servings**

2 scallions, cut into chunks
1 (1-inch) piece peeled, fresh ginger, cut into quarters
    (*see* Note, page 101)
2 garlic cloves, put through a garlic press
1 pound tuna steak, preferably sushi quality
2 teaspoons reduced-sodium soy sauce
2 teaspoons toasted sesame oil
6 cups mixed salad greens
1 cucumber, thinly sliced
1 carrot, shredded on the large holes of a box grater
2 tablespoons plus 2 teaspoons balsamic vinegar

1. Place the scallions and ginger on a cutting board and chop almost to a paste by rocking the blade of a chef's knife back and forth, rotating it slowly. Keep working in this fashion until the mixture is very finely chopped. Alternatively, place scallions and ginger in a small food processor and pulse until very finely chopped. Place the scallion mixture in a small bowl and mix with the pressed garlic to form a paste.

(*continued on next page*)

Seared Tuna Salad *(cont.)*

2. Brush both sides of the tuna with soy sauce. Massage the spice mixture into both sides and set aside for 5 minutes at room temperature.

3. Heat a large nonstick skillet or a seasoned cast-iron skillet over high heat until smoking. Add the oil, then slip tuna into the pan. (Be careful, it will splatter.) Cook 2 minutes, then turn and continue cooking to desired doneness, about 1 minute for rare, 2 minutes for medium rare, or 4 minutes for well done (*see* Note). Transfer to a cutting board and let rest at room temperature for 5 minutes.

4. Meanwhile, arrange 1½ cups salad greens and ¼ of the cucumber and carrot on each of four plates. Slice the tuna into ¼-inch-thick strips, cutting against the grain so the steak does not fall apart. Lay ¼ of the slices over each salad. Drizzle 2 teaspoons balsamic vinegar over each portion. Serve at once.

**NOTE:** You can watch the tuna cook from the sides—the pink will slowly disappear along the sides of the steak, roughly indicating how it's disappearing inside the piece of fish. But remember, the sides will cook more slowly than the interior, so use this only as a rough gauge, not a sure-fire test.

# Mexicali Layered Salad

**NUTRIENT ANALYSIS**

| | |
|---|---|
| Calories | 126.5 |
| Protein | 7 g |
| Carbohydrate | 23 g |
| Total Fat | 4 g |
| Saturated Fat | 0 g |
| Cholesterol | 13 mg |
| Fiber | 6 g |
| Sugars | 0 g |
| Sodium | 522 mg |

Each serving counts as
1 nonstarchy vegetable and
1 vegetarian protein (or 1 starchy
carbohydrate).

Think of this salad as a new take on the traditional seven-layer salad. It is both satisfying and bursting with flavor. What's more, it is abundant in fiber, which yields a number of weight- and appetite-controlling advantages (not to mention excellent digestive health). Using romaine lettuce in salads is a smart move since it is a vital source of folic acid, a vitamin now known to protect against many serious diseases and conditions.

**6 servings**

4 cups shredded romaine lettuce (about 6 large leaves)
2 large tomatoes, diced
1 cup canned pinto beans, drained and rinsed
1 small jicama, peeled and cut into matchsticks
3 medium scallions, thinly sliced
1 cup frozen corn, thawed
1 cup commercial salsa
1/2 cup fat-free sour cream
Juice of 1 lime
1/2 teaspoon ground cumin

1. Layer the lettuce, tomatoes, beans, jicama, scallions, and corn in a large glass casserole or a straight-sided salad bowl.

2. Combine the salsa, sour cream, lime juice, and cumin in a small bowl. Spoon the salsa mixture over the top of the salad, spreading it to cover. Serve by scooping up the salad with large salad tongs, gathering up all the layers and placing them on a plate.

# Curried Tabbouleh

**NUTRIENT ANALYSIS WITHOUT CHICKEN**

| | |
|---|---|
| Calories | 160 |
| Protein | 8 g |
| Carbohydrate | 33 g |
| Total Fat | 1 g |
| Saturated Fat | trace |
| Cholesterol | 0 mg |
| Fiber | 3 g |
| Sugars | 0 g |
| Sodium | 387 mg |

Each serving counts as 1 nonstarchy vegetable and 1 starchy carbohydrate.

**NUTRIENT ANALYSIS WITH CHICKEN**

| | |
|---|---|
| Calories | 246 |
| Protein | 24 g |
| Carbohydrate | 33 g |
| Total Fat | 3 g |
| Saturated Fat | 1 g |
| Cholesterol | 45 mg |
| Fiber | 3 g |
| Sugars | 0 |
| Sodium | 426 mg |

Each serving counts as 1 nonstarchy vegetable, 1 starchy carbohydrate, and 1 protein.

This low-fat, high-protein chicken salad draws its inspiration from Middle Eastern cuisine. It is an easy lunchtime solution for weight-conscious cooks, and, since it will keep in the refrigerator for up to three days, you can make it in advance so that it's ready when you are.

**4 servings**

1 cup medium-fine bulgur wheat
1 cup boiling water
1/4 cup fat-free plain yogurt
2 tablespoons freshly squeezed lemon juice
2 teaspoons curry powder
16 cherry tomatoes, halved
1 small red onion, finely chopped
2 ribs celery, thinly sliced
1/4 cup packed fresh cilantro leaves, finely chopped
1/4 cup packed fresh mint leaves, finely chopped
1 teaspoon salt
1/2 teaspoon freshly ground black pepper
1 1/2 cups cubed, cooked, skinless and boneless chicken breast
    (about 3/4 pound), optional (*see* Note)

1. Place the bulgur in a large bowl, stir in the boiling water, and set aside until water is absorbed and the bulgur is cool, about 30 minutes.

2. Meanwhile, combine the yogurt, lemon juice, and curry powder in a small bowl until creamy.

3. Fluff the bulgur with a fork, then add the tomatoes, onion, celery, cilantro, mint, salt, and pepper and stir well. Add the yogurt dressing and the chicken, if using, and toss to coat all the ingredients thoroughly. Cover and refrigerate for at least 1 hour to blend the flavors. The salad will keep, covered and refrigerated, for up to 3 days.

**NOTE:** Packaged cooked chicken breasts have shown up in many markets. Check the label to make sure yours aren't coated in spices that might conflict with the curry flavor in this dish. Also watch the sodium content. If the chicken has been injected with a saline solution, cut the salt from this recipe.

# Quinoa Grapefruit Salad

**NUTRIENT ANALYSIS**

| | |
|---|---|
| Calories | 211 |
| Protein | 5 g |
| Carbohydrate | 36 g |
| Total Fat | 5 g |
| Saturated Fat | 1 g |
| Cholesterol | 5 mg |
| Fiber | 3.5 mg |
| Sugars | 8 g |
| Sodium | 334 mg |

Each serving counts as
1 nonstarchy vegetable,
1 starchy carbohydrate, 2/3 fruit,
and 1/2 serving fat.

The seed of a leafy plant related to spinach, quinoa is what you might call a supergrain. It's unusually high in protein for a plant food, offering nearly the same amount as that from a serving of milk. In this recipe, it is paired with fruit, creating a genuinely healthy salad.

**6 servings**

2 cups water
$\frac{1}{2}$ teaspoon salt
1 cup dry quinoa, rinsed
1 large grapefruit
$\frac{1}{2}$ cup dried cherries or raisins
2 medium scallions, thinly sliced
4 ribs celery, thinly sliced
6 tablespoons commercial low-fat Caesar salad dressing

1. Bring water and salt to a boil in a medium saucepan set over high heat. Stir in the quinoa and return the mixture to a boil. Cover, reduce heat to low, and simmer until the water is absorbed and each tiny grain has a transparent halo around it, about 13 minutes. Remove from heat and set aside, covered, for 15 minutes.

2. Meanwhile, cut the grapefruit in half, not through the stem, but considering the stem to be the north pole and cutting through the grapefruit's equator. Use a grapefruit spoon to release the sections from the white pith and membranes in each half, letting the sections and any juice fall into a large bowl. Stir in the dried cherries or raisins, scallions, and celery.

3. Fluff the quinoa with a fork; add it to the bowl, and toss well. Pour in the dressing and toss well before serving.

**NOTE:** For a fancier presentation, serve the salad in hollowed tomatoes. Use a melon baller and core the tomatoes, starting at the stems and working upward, scooping out the flesh and seeds but taking care not to pierce the skins.

# Brown-Bag Shrimp

**NUTRIENT ANALYSIS**

| | |
|---|---|
| Calories | 149 |
| Protein | 8 g |
| Carbohydrate | 15 g |
| Total Fat | 7 g |
| Saturated Fat | 1 g |
| Cholesterol | 72 mg |
| Fiber | 3.5 g |
| Sugars | 0 g |
| Sodium | 392 mg |

Each serving counts as
1 nonstarchy vegetable and
1 protein.

This easy lunch is assembled quickly, without much fuss but with plenty of flavor. Buy frozen cooked shrimp in large bags in the freezer section of your market. A note here about common sense and safety: If you live in a hot climate, the shrimp should be stored in the refrigerator until you're ready to eat.

**1 serving**

4 or 5 large frozen cooked cocktail shrimp
    (about 12 to 15 shrimp per pound)
8 baby carrots
3 ribs celery, cut into 2-inch pieces
2 tablespoons commercial low-fat salad dressing or
    cocktail sauce

Place the frozen shrimp, carrots, and celery in a plastic container and seal it tightly. Place the salad dressing or cocktail sauce in a second small container. Let stand at room temperature no more than 2 hours, or refrigerated for up to 8 hours, until the shrimp are defrosted and ready to eat. Dip the shrimp, carrots, and celery in the dressing or cocktail sauce.

# The New BLT

| NUTRIENT ANALYSIS | |
| --- | --- |
| Calories | 253 |
| Protein | 13 g |
| Carbohydrate | 40 g |
| Total Fat | 9 g |
| Saturated Fat | 1 g |
| Cholesterol | 20 mg |
| Fiber | 7 g |
| Sugars | 6 g |
| Sodium | 801 mg |

Each serving counts as
1 nonstarchy vegetable,
2 starchy carbohydrates, and
1 protein.

BLTs are perennial favorites in our home, but we have learned to lighten them up considerably using the newer low-fat products on the market. This adaptation of the traditional favorite doesn't lose any of the flavor of the original, and tastes sensational.

**4 servings**

2 tablespoons Dijon or whole-grain mustard
1 tablespoon Miracle Whip Light or Miracle Whip Free
1/4 teaspoon maple extract
8 strips turkey bacon or meatless bacon
8 slices whole-grain bread, toasted (*see* Note 1)
4 romaine or red-leaf lettuce leaves, cut in half
1 large tomato, cut into 8 rounds

1. Combine the mustard, Miracle Whip, and maple extract in a small bowl and set aside.

2. Heat a large nonstick skillet over medium-high heat. Add the bacon and cook until crisp, turning once, about 2 minutes. Drain on a plate lined with paper towels.

3. Spread 1/4 of the mustard mixture over each of 4 slices of toast. Top each with 2 strips of bacon, 2 lettuce-leaf halves, and 2 slices of tomato, then second piece of toast. Serve at once. (*see* Note 2)

**NOTE 1:** If you want to save a bread serving for another time of day, you can make this sandwich open-faced, with only 1 slice of whole-grain bread as the base.

**NOTE 2:** For a packed lunch, keep all the ingredients separate until you're ready to eat so that the bread doesn't get soggy.

# Tuna Salad Wrap

**NUTRIENT ANALYSIS**

| | |
|---|---|
| Calories | 209 |
| Protein | 22 g |
| Carbohydrate | 22 g |
| Total Fat | 3 g |
| Saturated Fat | 1 g |
| Cholesterol | 36 mg |
| Fiber | 10 g |
| Sugars | .5 g |
| Sodium | 1,361 mg |

Each serving counts as
1 nonstarchy vegetable,
1 starchy carbohydrate,
and 1 protein.

Try something new for lunch—a wrap instead of a sandwich. With the high-nutrient densities of tuna and whole-wheat tortillas, you can take your nutrition to a much-improved level at lunchtime. This wrap is packable, but only if you keep the filling and the tortilla separate so that the tortilla doesn't get soggy over the course of the morning. Store the filling in the refrigerator so that the mayonnaise doesn't spoil.

**2 servings**

1 (6-ounce) can solid white tuna packed in water, drained
1 rib celery, minced
1 small dill pickle, minced
3 tablespoons fat-free mayonnaise or Miracle Whip Free
2 tablespoons finely chopped red onion
2 teaspoons freshly squeezed lemon juice
$1/2$ teaspoon dried dill, or 1 teaspoon packed fresh dill, minced
$1/4$ teaspoon salt
$1/4$ teaspoon freshly ground black pepper
2 fat-free whole-wheat tortillas

1. Combine the tuna, celery, pickle, mayonnaise, onion, lemon juice, dill, salt, and pepper in a medium bowl. Cover and store in the refrigerator for up to 24 hours.

2. To make the wrap, spoon about $1/2$ cup filling into each tortilla and roll closed.

# Grilled Vegetable Wrap

**NUTRIENT ANALYSIS**

| | |
|---|---|
| Calories | 166 |
| Protein | 8 g |
| Carbohydrate | 31 g |
| Total Fat | 2 g |
| Saturated Fat | trace |
| Cholesterol | 0 mg |
| Fiber | 14 g |
| Sugars | 0 g |
| Sodium | 309 mg |

Each serving counts as 1 nonstarchy vegetable, 1 starchy carbohydrate, and a negligible amount of vegetarian protein from the beans.

This vegetarian wrap holds the mayo and uses white bean spread as a nutritious, fat-free substitute. Whole-wheat tortillas are an example of a high-response cost, high-yield carbohydrate that allows a slower, more sustained release of glucose into your bloodstream than do low-response cost, low-yield carbs such as white bread. If you're grilling, do the vegetables the night before and refrigerate them, covered, until the next day. The spread can also be made on its own and served as a dip for celery and baby carrots. Covered and refrigerated, it will stay fresh up to 3 days.

**6 servings**

3 large zucchini, sliced lengthwise into ¼-inch-thick strips
2 medium red onions, sliced ¼-inch thick
1 cup canned white beans, drained and rinsed
1 jarred whole pimento, rinsed
1 tablespoon tahini (*see* Note)
1 teaspoon no-salt lemon pepper
1 teaspoon ground cumin
½ teaspoon salt
6 fat-free whole-wheat tortillas

1. Prepare a charcoal grill by making a bed of coals and placing the rack 4 to 6 inches above them, or heat a gas grill to high. Grill the zucchini strips and onion slices until browned and slightly soft, about 3 minutes, turning once. Transfer them to a platter and set aside.

2. Place the white beans, pimento, tahini, lemon pepper, cumin, and salt in a food processor fitted with the chopping blade, a small food processor, or a wide-bottomed blender. Process or blend until smooth, about 1 minute.

3. Spread 2¹/₂ tablespoons of the white bean puree onto each of the tortillas and top each one with ⅙ of the grilled vegetables. Roll tortillas closed and serve at once, or wrap each one tightly in plastic wrap and store at room temperature for 3 hours, or refrigerate up to 24 hours.

**NOTE:** *Tahini* is a paste made from toasted sesame seeds—sort of like the peanut butter of sesame seeds. If possible, buy it in bulk at a gourmet or health-food market so that you can ladle out exactly the amount you need. Or, buy it in glass jars so you can tell if it's discolored into dry, dark brown bands. If it has, don't use it. You can store tahini in the refrigerator, tightly covered, for up to 6 months.

# 5
# Entrées and Side Dishes

Sharing a meal with your family or someone you love carries the potential to be a tremendously healthy, constructive, positive, even intimate, experience. The trouble is, only a very few families in America sit down together for dinner anymore. Because we live in an era when we are so distracted so much of the time—going to work, picking up kids from practice, coming home, eating a fast dinner, heading to the remote control or a book—there is little, if any, time amidst this blur of hyperactivity and diversion to spend meaningfully with those who share our lives. We've gotten used to this chaotic and harried style of living.

What I would like to challenge you to do is to change these realities and behaviors. Find ways of being together at meals that work for your family, whether that means planning a few nights during the week when everyone is home, or determining a doable length of time for dinner. (Who says the dinner hour has to last an hour?) Sitting down as a family for meals may also be the most important communicating you can do all day. Research shows that the more often you have dinner together, the less likely your children will take up smoking, drinking, or using illegal drugs. It is also one of the best ways I know for you and your spouse to teach your children healthier eating habits and better social skills. In short, the family meal can help keep your family close, connected—and healthy.

Let this chapter, with its nutritious and tasty entrées and side dishes, be the starting point for preparing dinners your family will love and, simultaneously, creating a nurturing atmosphere at mealtime. There is something for everyone here, from main dishes made with meat, poultry, or fish to those that are purely vegetarian.

So, help those you love to thrive at every possible level—physically, emotionally, and socially. Take some of the time and energy you might ordinarily spend on other things and invest it in making your family time something better.

# Herbed Beef Tenderloin

| NUTRIENT ANALYSIS | |
| --- | --- |
| Calories | 318 |
| Protein | 43 g |
| Carbohydrate | 1 g |
| Total Fat | 14 g |
| Saturated Fat | 5 g |
| Cholesterol | 127 mg |
| Fiber | trace |
| Sugars | 0 g |
| Sodium | 212 mg |

Each serving counts as 1 protein.

If you want your weight to be lower than it has been in the past, it is best to select lower-fat cuts of beef, such as tenderloin. Preparing tenderloin with fresh herbs is the best way to go, since the meat takes on the special flavors with which it is paired.

### 9 servings

1/4 cup fresh flat-leaf parsley, finely chopped
2 tablespoons fresh tarragon leaves, finely chopped
1 tablespoon fresh thyme leaves, minced
1/2 teaspoon salt
1/4 teaspoon freshly ground black pepper
3 pounds beef tenderloin, trimmed of exterior fat

2 garlic cloves, slivered

¼ cup Dijon mustard (smooth, not coarse-grained)

1. Preheat oven to 400°F. Combine the parsley, tarragon, thyme, salt, and pepper on a large plate.

2. Using a paring knife, make as many tiny slits as you have garlic slivers across the entire rounded surface of the tenderloin, but not the ends. Place a garlic sliver in each slit. Smear the tenderloin, including the ends, evenly with the mustard; roll meat in the herb mixture, pressing to make sure herbs adhere; then place it in a shallow roasting pan or a broiler pan.

3. Roast to medium rare, or until an instant-read meat thermometer inserted into the center of the tenderloin registers 135°F, about 50 minutes; or to medium, until an instant-read meat thermometer registers 150°F, about 1 hour. (Check the temperature after 40 minutes in the oven to avoid overcooking the meat.) Let stand 10 minutes before carving.

**NOTE:** Many chefs determine how well done a piece of meat is by pressing it with a finger. You can learn this technique by holding one hand out in front of you. Rare meat feels like the excess flesh in the curve between your index finger and thumb when both are relaxed. Medium rare feels like the excess flesh just under your little finger, along the side of your hand. Medium feels about like the fleshy part of your hand between your thumb and index finger, about 1 inch down from where you tested for rare. And well done feels about like the center of your wrist. While taking the temperature is the best and most accurate guide, you don't have to poke the tenderloin with the instant-read thermometer every time—a quick touch will let you know when you're within shooting distance and it's time to start working with the thermometer.

# Pot Roast Southern Style

| NUTRIENT ANALYSIS | |
| --- | --- |
| Calories | 308 |
| Protein | 46 g |
| Carbohydrate | 12 g |
| Total Fat | 7 g |
| Saturated Fat | 2 g |
| Cholesterol | 104 mg |
| Fiber | 3 g |
| Sugars | 0 g |
| Sodium | 347 mg |

Each serving counts as 1 protein.

One of the memories that emerges from my growing-up years is the roast beef that my mother—Granma, as we all call her—fixed for our family. The version below is prepared with eye of the round, a less fatty choice than the usual chuck or brisket used in most pot roasts.

**6 servings**

1 teaspoon canola or vegetable oil
2 pounds eye round of beef, trimmed of any visible fat
2 large carrots, sliced into $1/2$-inch-thick disks (about 2 cups)
2 large parsnips, peeled and sliced into $1/2$-inch-thick disks
    (about 2 cups)
1 large rib celery, thinly sliced (about 1 cup)
1 teaspoon dried thyme
1 teaspoon sweet paprika
1 teaspoon dry mustard
$1/2$ teaspoon salt
$1/4$ teaspoon freshly ground black pepper
1 ($14^{1}/2$ ounce) can no-salt, fat-free beef broth
3 tablespoons prepared horseradish, preferably white
    (*see* Note 1)

1. Preheat oven to 350°F.

2. Heat the oil in a large ovenproof saucepan with a lid (*see* Note 2) set over medium heat. Add beef and brown on all sides, turning as necessary, about 3 minutes. Transfer to a plate and set aside.

3. Add carrots, parsnips, and celery to the pan. Cook, stirring often, until softened, about 2 minutes. Add thyme, paprika, mustard, salt, and pepper. Stir well, then cook until aromatic, about 20 seconds. Pour broth into pan, stir to scrape up any browned bits on the bottom, and bring to a simmer. Meanwhile, spread horseradish over top of roast.

4. Return beef to pan, horseradish side up. Cover pan, place in preheated oven, and bake for at least 2 hours, or up to $2^1/2$ hours, until fork tender.

**NOTE 1:** Prepared horseradish is available in the refrigerator case of most supermarkets, usually alongside the cold cuts. Use mild or spicy, depending on your preference, but check the sodium content. If you're on a reduced-sodium diet, omit the salt in this recipe.

**NOTE 2:** Most saucepans can handle oven temperatures up to 425°F, but many of their handles can't. If yours has a wooden, rubber, or composite handle, wrap the handle tightly in aluminum foil to protect it. And, in all cases, remove any slip-on handle covers before placing the saucepan in the oven. The same is also true for the handle on the lid.

# Beef and Broccoli Stir-Fry

**NUTRIENT ANALYSIS**

| | |
|---|---:|
| Calories | 176 |
| Protein | 21 g |
| Carbohydrate | 9 g |
| Total Fat | 6 g |
| Saturated Fat | 1.5 g |
| Cholesterol | 50 mg |
| Fiber | 3 g |
| Sugars | 1 g |
| Sodium | 326 mg |

Each serving counts as 1 protein
and 1 nonstarchy vegetable.

It is a well-known medical fact that broccoli and other cruciferous vegetables, such as cauliflower, cabbage, and Brussels sprouts, are cancer fighters. Every bite of these vegetables contains healthy doses of protective phytonutrients. One way to make broccoli more appealing to the vegetable haters in your family is to add it to stir-fry dishes like this one. Not only will the broccoli taste better, but many of the antioxidants and other beneficial plant substances it contains will be more easily absorbed by the body when eaten with the small amount of healthy oil that is part of the preparation. Like all red meat, sirloin is an excellent reservoir of iron, which is essential for building body-firming muscle and healthy blood. Despite the nutritional payoffs of red meat, however, you should go easy on the amount you eat. Restricting your consumption of red meat to a few times a month guards against eating an excess of saturated fat. Stir-fry dishes cook quickly, so have all your ingredients prepped before you start cooking.

**4 servings**

2 teaspoons peanut or vegetable oil
2 tablespoons peeled and minced fresh ginger (*see* Note 1)
2 medium scallions, minced
2 garlic cloves, minced
1/4 teaspoon crushed red-pepper flakes
Zest of 1 orange, thinly sliced (*see* Note 2)
1/2 pound boneless sirloin steak, trimmed of any fat around
    the rim and thinly sliced
2 cups fresh broccoli florets, or 1 (10-ounce) bag frozen broccoli
    florets, thawed

1 red bell pepper, cored, seeded, and chopped
2 tablespoons reduced-sodium soy sauce
2 tablespoons rice wine vinegar or white wine vinegar
1 teaspoon cornstarch whisked with 1 tablespoon water

1. Heat the oil in a large nonstick wok or large nonstick skillet set over medium-high heat. Add the ginger, scallions, and garlic; cook, tossing and stirring, until fragrant, about 30 seconds. Add red-pepper flakes and orange zest and cook 20 seconds longer.

2. Slip the sirloin strips into the pan and cook, stirring and tossing, until lightly browned, about 2 minutes. Add the broccoli and bell pepper; continue tossing and stirring until slightly softened but still crunchy, about 1 minute.

3. Pour in the soy sauce and vinegar and bring to a boil, stirring constantly. Add cornstarch mixture and cook, stirring, until thickened, about 15 seconds. Immediately remove from heat (do not let the cornstarch mixture continue to boil). Let stand 1 minute before serving.

**NOTE 1:** Look for fresh ginger in the produce section of your market. It should be firm, not mushy, with a dry, papery skin that must be removed before the inner fibers can be minced. A vegetable peeler works well for this.

**NOTE 2:** You can remove the zest (that is, the film-thin, colored skin of an orange, lemon, or lime in which the oil is concentrated) with a citrus zester, available at most gourmet stores or outlets online, or with the large holes of a box grater, provided you do not press the fruit too hard against the grater and thereby remove the bitter, white pith as well.

# Lean Meatloaf

**NUTRIENT ANALYSIS**

| | |
|---|---|
| Calories | 244 |
| Protein | 22 g |
| Carbohydrate | 10 g |
| Total Fat | 13 g |
| Saturated Fat | 5 g |
| Cholesterol | 70 mg |
| Fiber | 2 g |
| Sugars | 0 g |
| Sodium | 321 mg |

Each serving counts as 1 protein and 1 nonstarchy vegetable.

What you will find in this recipe is essentially a new spin on an old favorite—a low-fat, infinitely healthier way to prepare a meatloaf that is also infused with flavor. The ground mushrooms supply the moisture that leaner cuts of ground beef and veal usually lack, ensuring a juicier meatloaf.

**6 servings**

1 pound button mushrooms, brushed of dirt
$3/4$ pound ground round of beef
$1/2$ pound ground veal
$1/2$ cup old-fashioned rolled oats (*not* quick-cooking)
$1/4$ cup pasteurized egg substitute
2 tablespoons minced dry onion
2 teaspoons rubbed sage
2 teaspoons dried thyme
1 teaspoon salt
$1/2$ teaspoon garlic powder
$1/4$ teaspoon freshly ground black pepper
$1/4$ teaspoon cayenne pepper, optional
1 medium tomato, sliced paper thin

1. Preheat oven to 350°F.

2. Place the mushrooms in a food processor fitted with the chopping blade. Pulse once or twice to chop lightly, then process until ground to the consistency of very coarse meal. If you don't have a food processor, chop the mushrooms with a large knife until they look like fine meal, moving the knife all over the cutting board as you rock it back and forth.

3. Scoop a handful of the ground mushrooms into some paper towels. Form a closed packet, then squeeze over the sink to remove all excess moisture. You may have to turn the packet several ways to get all the moisture out of the mushrooms, particularly if your hands are small. Place the squeezed mushrooms in a large bowl and repeat with the remaining ground mushrooms, working in batches.

4. Making sure your hands are scrupulously clean, crumble the ground round and ground veal into the bowl, stir well, and add the oats, egg substitute, onion, sage, thyme, salt, garlic powder, black pepper, and cayenne pepper, if using. Work the mixture through your fingers, squeezing gently until ingredients are well blended and of a uniform consistency.

5. Shape the mixture into a small loaf, about 8 inches long, like a small football. Place the loaf in a medium baking dish and lay tomato slices over the top, overlapping as necessary to form a line of slices along the length of the loaf.

6. Bake until well browned and firm, about 50 minutes; an instant-read meat thermometer inserted into the thickest part of the loaf should read 165°F. Let stand 5 minutes at room temperature before slicing and serving.

# No-Fry Chicken-Fried Steak

| NUTRIENT ANALYSIS | |
|---|---|
| Calories | 358 |
| Protein | 46 g |
| Carbohydrate | 27 g |
| Total Fat | 7 g |
| Saturated Fat | 3 g |
| Cholesterol | 104 mg |
| Fiber | 3.5 mg |
| Sugars | 0 g |
| Sodium | 576 mg |

Each serving counts as 1 protein and approximately 1 starchy carbohydrate.

I confess that my all-time favorite food is chicken-fried steak, a popular dish in Texas, served practically everywhere, from truck stops to country cooking restaurants. It is estimated that eight hundred thousand chicken-fried steaks are eaten in the Lone Star state every day. As much as two cups of fat are normally required to shallow-fry chicken-fried steak, however, so eating this Texas specialty as a matter of habit is sure to invite plenty of unwelcome pounds. In this version, most of the fat has been eliminated, and the calories pared considerably, all without sacrificing flavor.

**4 servings**

4 top round or sirloin tip steaks (about 5 ounces each)
1 teaspoon meat tenderizer
1 cup low-fat buttermilk
Nonstick spray
1 cup oat flour, or 1 cup uncooked old-fashioned rolled oats, finely ground in a food processor or blender (*not* quick-cooking oats)
2 teaspoons sweet paprika
1 teaspoon onion powder
1 teaspoon salt
$1/2$ teaspoon garlic powder
$1/4$ teaspoon freshly ground black pepper
$1/8$ teaspoon cayenne pepper, optional

1. Place the steaks between two large sheets of wax paper. Using a meat mallet or the bottom of a large, heavy saucepan, pound the steaks to $1/4$-inch thickness. Remove the top sheet of wax pa-

per, prick the meat with a fork at ½-inch intervals, and season evenly across the pricked surface with meat tenderizer. Peel steaks off the bottom sheet of wax paper and place in a large shallow roasting pan (they can overlap). Pour the buttermilk over the steaks and marinate at room temperature for 30 minutes, turning occasionally to coat thoroughly in buttermilk.

2. Meanwhile, position the rack in the bottom third of the oven and preheat to 400°F. Spray a large, shallow roasting pan or a large, rimmed baking sheet with nonstick spray. On a large plate, combine the oat flour or ground oats with the paprika, onion powder, salt, garlic powder, black pepper, and cayenne, if using, mixing well.

3. Dredge the buttermilk-coated steaks in oat flour mixture, then place in the prepared baking pan. Spray them lightly with nonstick spray. Bake until firm but tender when pierced with a fork and lightly browned, about 30 minutes.

# Italian Roast Pork Loin

**NUTRIENT ANALYSIS**

| | |
|---|---|
| Calories | 259 |
| Protein | 33 g |
| Carbohydrate | 1 g |
| Total Fat | 13 g |
| Saturated Fat | 4 g |
| Cholesterol | 92 mg |
| Fiber | 1 g |
| Sugars | 0 g |
| Sodium | 242 mg |

Each serving counts as 1 protein.

Enjoying pork on occasion will not send the scales soaring, so long as you choose the healthier, lean cuts such as loin or tenderloin, which compare favorably to skinless chicken in terms of fat and calorie content. This hearty, no-fuss recipe revamps the classic Italian rendition without tons of fat.

**8 servings**

1 tablespoon no-salt lemon pepper
2 teaspoons fennel seeds
2 teaspoons dried oregano
2 teaspoons dried rosemary
1 teaspoon salt
1 tablespoon olive oil
3 garlic cloves, mashed or put through a garlic press
1 (2½-pound) pork loin, trimmed of all exterior fat

1. Preheat oven to 325°F. Combine the lemon pepper, fennel seeds, oregano, rosemary, and salt in a small bowl; set aside. Combine the olive oil and mashed garlic in a second small bowl. Rub the olive oil mixture evenly over the pork loin, coating it thoroughly. Sprinkle the herb mixture over the entire pork loin. Place in a shallow roasting pan, broiler pan, or shallow baking dish.

2. Roast until golden brown. An instant-read meat thermometer inserted into the thickest part of the loin should register 160°F for medium, about 65 minutes, or 170° for well done, about 1 hour and 15 minutes.

# Pork and Black-Bean Stew

| NUTRIENT ANALYSIS | |
| --- | --- |
| Calories | 291 |
| Protein | 30 g |
| Carbohydrate | 24.5 g |
| Total Fat | 10 g |
| Saturated Fat | 3 g |
| Cholesterol | 67 mg |
| Fiber | 8 g |
| Sugars | 1 g |
| Sodium | 586 mg |

Each serving counts as 1 protein and 1 starchy carbohydrate.

Pork is an efficient source of protein and an excellent provider of important minerals. Like all our meat recipes, this stew—a healthy rendition of a Texas classic—calls for a lean cut, trimmed of all exterior fat in order to slash fat and calories even further. Paired with fiber-rich black beans and other vegetables, the stew provides a near-balanced meal, all in one convenient dish.

**4 servings**

2 teaspoons olive oil
1 medium onion, chopped, or ¾ cup frozen chopped onion
3 garlic cloves, minced
1 pound boneless pork loin, trimmed of any exterior fat, cut into
    ½-inch cubes
2 tablespoons chili powder
1 teaspoon ground cumin
1 teaspoon ground cinnamon
1 pickled jalapeño pepper, seeded and minced (*see* Note)
1½ cups water
1 (15-ounce) can black beans, drained and rinsed
2 tablespoons corn grits, old-fashioned or quick-cooking
¼ cup chopped fresh cilantro
1 tablespoon freshly squeezed lime juice

1. Heat the oil in a large nonstick saucepan set over medium heat. Add the onion and garlic and cook, stirring, until softened, about 2 minutes. Add the cubed pork and cook, stirring often, until browned, about 4 minutes.

*(continued on next page)*

Pork and Black-Bean Stew *(cont.)*

2. Add chili powder, cumin, cinnamon, and jalapeño; cook until aromatic, about 20 seconds. Pour in the water and beans and stir well to scrape up any browned bits on the bottom of the pan. Bring to a boil, cover, reduce heat to low, and simmer very slowly for 15 minutes.

3. Stir in the grits and cook until thickened and intense, about 15 more minutes, stirring quite often to prevent sticking. Stir in cilantro and lime juice; serve at once.

**NOTE:** A jarred, pickled jalapeño, packed in a vinegary brine, will give this dish a nice sparkle. Wash your hands carefully after working with the pepper—if you touch your eyes, you'll be in for a nasty chili burn. For a far more fiery dish, don't seed the pepper before you mince it.

# Grilled Southwestern Pork Tenderloin

| NUTRIENT ANALYSIS | |
|---|---:|
| Calories | 201 |
| Protein | 33 g |
| Carbohydrate | 3 g |
| Total Fat | 7 g |
| Saturated Fat | 2 g |
| Cholesterol | 90 mg |
| Fiber | 1 g |
| Sugars | 0 g |
| Sodium | 127 mg |

Each serving counts as 1 protein.

I am passionate about grilling, not just because it is a fast and effective way to cook, but also because it is a cooking method that virtually guarantees a lean and flavorful outcome. Try this simple marinade of herbs and liquids on pork the next time you fire up your grill.

**4 servings**

2 tablespoons freshly squeezed lime juice
1 tablespoon chili powder
1 tablespoon Worcestershire sauce

1½ teaspoons ground cumin
1 teaspoon liquid smoke (*see* Note, page 141)
1¼ pound pork tenderloin, trimmed of any exterior fat

1. Place the lime juice, chili powder, Worcestershire sauce, cumin, and liquid smoke in a resealable plastic bag. Drop in the pork tenderloin and seal the bag, pressing out any excess air. Rub the sides of the bag between your hands, rubbing the spices into the meat. Refrigerate for at least 2 hours or up to 18 hours, rubbing the bag to distribute the spices at least twice, if not several more times.

2. Prepare the charcoal grill by making a bed of coals and placing the rack 4 to 6 inches above them, or heat a gas grill to high. Remove the pork tenderloin from the bag and grill over direct, high heat, turning it onto all four sides, until browned, 14 to 17 minutes. An instant-read meat thermometer inserted into the thickest part of the tenderloin should read 160°F for medium and 170°F for well done. Let stand off the heat for 5 minutes before carving.

3. Alternatively, preheat broiler. Broil the tenderloin about 5 inches from the heat in a shallow metal roasting or broiler pan, turning it onto all four sides, until brown and cooked to the appropriate temperature, about 20 minutes.

# Pork Lo Mein

| | |
|---|---|
| Calories | 290 |
| Protein | 30 g |
| Carbohydrate | 24 g |
| Total Fat | 8 g |
| Saturated Fat | 2 g |
| Cholesterol | 94 mg |
| Fiber | 2 g |
| Sugars | 1 g |
| Sodium | 335 mg |

Each serving counts as 1 protein, 1 starchy carbohydrate, and 1 nonstarchy vegetable.

Lean and versatile pork tenderloin can be used in many ethnic dishes and matched with dozens of other ingredients. This version of lo mein is a nutritious, one-dish meal, loaded with protein, carbohydrates, vitamins, and minerals. It takes just minutes to fix as long as you do your food prep ahead of time. If you are not familiar with five-spice powder, it is a blend of ground Asian spices—namely cinnamon, star anise, fennel, ginger, and cloves. You can find it in the spice aisle of most supermarkets.

**4 servings**

2 teaspoons peanut oil
2 garlic cloves, slivered
3 tablespoons peeled and minced fresh ginger
   (*see* Note, page 101)
3/4 pound pork tenderloin, trimmed of exterior fat and shredded
   (*see* Note)
1/2 teaspoon five-spice powder
3 medium scallions, cut into 1-inch pieces
2 cups mung bean sprouts (about 8 ounces)
2 cups cooked Japanese somen noodles, Chinese egg noodles
   (enriched), or udon noodles
2 tablespoons reduced-sodium soy sauce

1. Heat the peanut oil in a large nonstick wok or skillet set over medium-high heat. Add the garlic and ginger and cook, stirring constantly, until fragrant, about 20 seconds. Add the shredded pork and cook, tossing and stirring, until browned, about 2 minutes.

2. Sprinkle the five-spice powder over the ingredients and toss well. Add scallions and cook, stirring constantly, until softened, about 2 minutes. Add bean sprouts and cooked noodles. Continue cooking, tossing and stirring, until all the ingredients are heated through, about 1 minute. Add soy sauce and cook just until it is absorbed, about 20 seconds. Serve at once.

**NOTE:** To shred a pork tenderloin, cut it into thin rounds, no more than $\frac{1}{4}$-inch thick, then slice rounds into thin strips, like matchsticks.

# Grilled Greek Lamb Chops

| NUTRIENT ANALYSIS | |
|---|---:|
| Calories | 223 |
| Protein | 32 g |
| Carbohydrate | 2 g |
| Total Fat | 9 g |
| Saturated Fat | 4 g |
| Cholesterol | 96 mg |
| Fiber | 1 g |
| Sugars | 0 g |
| Sodium | 426 mg |

Each serving counts as 1 protein.

If you are accustomed to eating mostly beef, do something that is not part of your regular mealtime routine: Try lamb. It is easy to prepare and has an affinity for an array of herbs and spices, which is why you find it on so many European and Mediterranean tables. This recipe uses a blend of spices that embody the flavors of Greece. Serve it with a simple salad of sliced tomatoes and cucumbers dressed with lemon juice and a small amount of coarse salt.

**4 servings**

2 garlic cloves, mashed or put through a garlic press
1 tablespoon dried oregano
2 teaspoons dried thyme
2 teaspoons grated lemon zest (*see* Note, page 101)
1 teaspoon salt
$^1/_2$ teaspoon freshly ground black pepper
8 (1-inch-thick) loin or rib lamb chops (about $2^1/_2$ ounces each), trimmed of any exterior fat

1. Combine the garlic, oregano, thyme, lemon zest, salt, and pepper in a small bowl. Rub the mixture evenly into both sides of the lamb chops. Place the chops in a shallow roasting pan, broiler pan, or baking dish, cover, and refrigerate 1 hour.

2. Prepare a charcoal grill by making a bed of coals and placing the rack 4 to 6 inches above them, or heat a gas grill to high. Grill the chops over direct high heat, turning them once, until browned, 6 to 9 minutes. An instant-read meat thermometer inserted into the thickest part of the chops should read 135°F for

medium rare and 150°F for well done. Let stand off the heat for 5 minutes before carving.

3. Alternatively, preheat broiler. Broil the chops 5 inches from the heat in a metal roasting or broiler pan, turning them once, until brown and cooked to appropriate temperature, about 8 to 11 minutes.

# Better than Classic Shepherd's Pie

An English casserole, shepherd's pie is the ultimate comfort food in winter. It provides a healthy meal, made with high-response cost, high-yield proteins and carbohydrates. If you use frozen vegetables, do not thaw the peas and carrots or the chopped onion.

**4 servings**

2 medium baking potatoes, preferably russets (8 ounces each), peeled and cut into 1-inch cubes

2 teaspoons canola oil

1 medium onion, chopped, or $3/4$ cup frozen chopped onion

1 pound extra-lean ground beef

2 teaspoons dried thyme

2 teaspoons Worcestershire sauce

2 teaspoons whole-wheat flour

$1/2$ cup no-salt, fat-free vegetable broth

1 cup frozen peas and carrots, or $1/2$ cup peas mixed with $1/2$ cup diced carrots

$1/2$ cup fat-free milk

2 teaspoons Dijon mustard

$1/2$ teaspoon onion powder

$1/4$ teaspoon salt

$1/4$ teaspoon freshly ground black pepper

$1/2$ teaspoon sweet paprika

1. Preheat oven to 350°F.

2. Bring a large pot of water to a boil over high heat. Add the cubed potatoes and cook until tender when pierced with a knife, about 12 minutes.

3. Meanwhile, prepare the filling: Heat the oil in a large non-stick skillet or high-sided sauté pan set over medium heat. Add the onion and cook, stirring, until softened, about 2 minutes. Crumble in the ground beef and cook, stirring frequently, until lightly browned, about 2 minutes. Stir in the thyme and Worcestershire sauce, then sprinkle the whole-wheat flour evenly over the ingredients in the pan. Cook 10 seconds, then stir well and continue cooking 15 seconds longer, just until the flour loses its raw taste. Stir in ¼ cup broth and cook, stirring, until thickened, about 30 seconds. Finally, stir in peas and carrots, then spread into an 8-inch-square baking dish.

4. When the potatoes are tender, drain and transfer to a large bowl. Add the milk, mustard, onion powder, salt, pepper, and remaining ¼ cup broth. Mash with a potato masher or an electric mixer at medium speed until creamy and light. Spread the potato mixture over the ground beef, forming a topping that extends all the way to the edges of the baking dish. Lightly seal the mashed potatoes to the baking dish by pressing down at the edges. Sprinkle with paprika.

5. Bake until the potatoes are golden at the edges and there's a little steam coming up through them, about 25 minutes. Let stand 5 minutes at room temperature before serving.

# Herb Roasted Chicken

**NUTRIENT ANALYSIS**

| | |
|---|---|
| Calories | 184 |
| Protein | 31 g |
| Carbohydrate | 3 g |
| Total Fat | 5 g |
| Saturated Fat | 1 g |
| Cholesterol | 85 mg |
| Fiber | 1 g |
| Sugars | 0 g |
| Sodium | 241 mg |

Each serving counts as 1 protein.

In our home, we eat chicken several nights of the week and, admittedly, this regular standby does get boring at times, which is why we like to try new methods of preparing it. This recipe transforms everyday chicken into a true masterpiece. It is not only good, it is great.

**8 servings**

¼ cup packed fresh sage leaves, finely chopped
2 tablespoons fresh flat-leaf parsley leaves, finely chopped
1 tablespoon fresh thyme leaves, minced
1 teaspoon salt
½ teaspoon finely ground black pepper
1 (5-pound) roasting chicken, giblets and any excess fat removed
1 lemon, quartered
1 onion, quartered
1 rib celery, sliced into 2-inch pieces

1. Preheat oven to 425°F. In a small bowl, combine the sage, parsley, thyme, salt, and pepper and set aside.

2. Starting at the large opening of the chicken and working back over the breast, run your fingers between the skin and the meat to create a pocket over each side of the breast. Slip ¼ of the herb mixture into each pocket, massaging the herbs into the meat but taking care not to tear the skin. Make a small slit in each thigh. Separate the skin from the meat by again running a finger through the slits and working the skin loose. Slip the remaining spice mixture into the thigh pockets, again massaging the herbs into the meat without breaking the skin. Finally, squeeze the lemon juice into the larger cavity of the bird and rub your hands

over the interior to coat it with the juice. Place the lemon wedges, onion quarters, and celery inside the large cavity.

3. Place the chicken breast-side up in a shallow roasting pan, broiler pan, or baking dish fitted with a rack or other device designed to keep it out of the rendered fat that will pool in the pan. Roast until golden brown and an instant-read meat thermometer inserted into the thickest part of the thigh registers 165°F, about 1 hour and 30 minutes. Let stand 5 minutes at room temperature before carving.

# Southern Oven-Fried Chicken

| NUTRIENT ANALYSIS | |
| --- | --- |
| Calories | 265 |
| Protein | 38 g |
| Carbohydrate | 17 g |
| Total Fat | 5 g |
| Saturated Fat | 1 g |
| Cholesterol | 96 mg |
| Fiber | 2 g |
| Sugars | 2 g |
| Sodium | 218 mg |

Each serving counts as 1 protein and approximately ⅓ starchy carbohydrate.

If you are a fried chicken lover, here is a way to experience the sensory gratification of eating it without abandoning your weight loss goals. Once you incorporate this greatly reduced-fat version of the Southern classic into your regular meal plan, trust me, you will lose your preference for regular fried chicken.

**6 servings**

Nonstick spray
Brine: 2½ cups water mixed with ¼ cup salt and
       ¼ cup apple-cider vinegar
3 very large skinless and boneless chicken breasts (about 10 to
       12 ounces each), halved, or 6 small skinless and boneless
       chicken breasts (about 5 to 6 ounces each)
1 cup Grape-Nuts, or other crunchy whole-wheat and barley
       cereal
1¼ teaspoons chili powder
1 teaspoon ground cumin
1 teaspoon dried thyme
1 teaspoon onion powder
¼ teaspoon garlic powder
1 large egg white beaten with 2 tablespoons water until foamy

1. Heat oven to 350°F. Spray a large, rimmed baking sheet with nonstick spray; set aside.

2. Add the chicken breasts to the brine mixture, stir, and set aside at room temperature for 15 minutes. (Brining the breasts will keep them plump during baking.) Mix the Grape-Nuts, chili powder, cumin, thyme, onion powder, and garlic powder on a large plate until well blended.

3. Drain and rinse the breasts and blot dry with paper towels. Dip one piece in the egg white mixture, let the excess slip back into bowl, then roll the breast in the cereal mixture, lightly coating all sides. Place on the prepared baking sheet and repeat with remaining breasts.

4. Bake until crunchy and brown, about 25 or 30 minutes. Let stand at room temperature 2 to 3 minutes before serving.

# Apricot-Glazed Chicken Breasts

| NUTRIENT ANALYSIS | |
| --- | --- |
| Calories | 222 |
| Protein | 36 g |
| Carbohydrate | 5 g |
| Total Fat | 6 g |
| Saturated Fat | 1.4 g |
| Cholesterol | 96 mg |
| Fiber | 1 g |
| Sugars | trace |
| Sodium | 127 mg |

Each serving counts as 1 protein.

Chicken has a well-known affinity for fruit that opens the door to lots of options for preparation. Here, the apricots shake the flavor of the chicken awake. A note of caution: Read the label on packaged frozen chicken breasts; some of them are injected with a saline solution and thus contain a hefty amount of sodium. Be sure to use fresh rosemary, not dried, because the dried herb does not have time to soften in the glaze and will remain too spiky.

**6 servings**

10 dried apricot halves, preferably the tart California variety
1 cup no-salt, fat-free vegetable broth
2 teaspoons chopped fresh rosemary
2 teaspoons apple-cider vinegar
2 teaspoons reduced-sodium soy sauce
1/4 teaspoon freshly ground black pepper
2 teaspoons olive oil

*(continued on next page)*

Apricot-Glazed Chicken Breasts *(cont.)*

3 very large skinless and boneless chicken breasts (about 10 to 12 ounces each), halved, or 6 small skinless and boneless chicken breasts (about 5 to 6 ounces each)

1. Preheat oven to 375°F.

2. Bring the apricots, broth, rosemary, vinegar, soy sauce, and pepper to a boil in a small saucepan set over medium-high heat. Remove from heat, cover, and set aside until the mixture cools and apricots soften, about 10 minutes.

3. Pour the apricot mixture into a food processor fitted with the chopping blade, or a large blender. Add the olive oil and puree, scraping down the sides of the bowl as necessary.

4. Place chicken breasts in a roasting pan or baking dish large enough to hold them comfortably in one layer. Spread the apricot glaze over the breasts. Bake 10 minutes undisturbed, then bake another 15 minutes, basting with the pan juices every 5 minutes, until the chicken is cooked through and lightly browned. Let stand at room temperature 5 minutes before serving.

# Moroccan Chicken

This recipe draws inspiration from Moroccan cuisine to create a chicken dish with big, bold flavors. It uses Brussels sprouts, another vegetable considered to be especially protective against cancer. If you want to give this dish a fiery blast, toss in a jalapeño pepper, finely diced, along with the spices.

**NUTRIENT ANALYSIS**

| | |
|---|---|
| Calories | 297 |
| Protein | 39 g |
| Carbohydrate | 24 g |
| Total Fat | 5 g |
| Saturated Fat | 1 g |
| Cholesterol | 96 g |
| Fiber | 2.5 g |
| Sugars | 7 g |
| Sodium | 374 mg |

Each serving counts as 1 protein,
1 nonstarchy vegetable, and
1 starchy carbohydrate.

## 4 servings

2 very large skinless and boneless chicken breasts (about 10 to
    12 ounces each), cut into 1-inch pieces, or 4 small skinless
    and boneless chicken breasts (about 5 to 6 ounces each),
    cut into 1-inch pieces
2 teaspoons ground cumin
1 teaspoon ground cinnamon
$3/4$ teaspoon salt
$1/2$ teaspoon ground turmeric
$1/2$ teaspoon ground ginger
$1/2$ teaspoon freshly ground black pepper
1 large sweet potato, peeled and cut into 1-inch cubes (2 cups)
20 fresh Brussels sprouts (about 12 ounces), tough outer leaves
    removed, or frozen Brussels sprouts, thawed
$1/4$ cup raisins
$1/4$ cup no-salt, fat-free vegetable broth

1. Preheat oven to 375°F.

2. Place the chicken pieces in a large bowl and toss them with the
cumin, cinnamon, salt, turmeric, ginger, and pepper until well
coated. Transfer to a 3-quart ovenproof casserole or Dutch oven.
Mix in the sweet potato, Brussels sprouts, raisins, and broth.

3. Cover and bake, tossing and stirring two or three times, until
the chicken is cooked through and the dish is very fragrant, about
1 hour. Let stand at room temperature 5 minutes before serving.

# Bistro Chicken Stew

**NUTRIENT ANALYSIS**

| | |
|---|---|
| Calories | 363 |
| Protein | 40 g |
| Carbohydrate | 37 g |
| Total Fat | 7 g |
| Saturated Fat | 2 g |
| Cholesterol | 96 mg |
| Fiber | 6 g |
| Sugars | 0 g |
| Sodium | 340 mg |

Each serving counts as 1 protein, 1 nonstarchy vegetable, and 1 fruit.

This classic French dish, refitted for high-level nutrition, showcases it all: chicken, vegetables, and fruit. The result is a main meal that delivers nutrition payoffs of high protein and high fiber. Fiber, of course, is the substance in fruits and vegetables that has been cited as a possible preventative for obesity, heart disease, diabetes, and some cancers.

**4 servings**

2 teaspoons olive oil
8 small skinless and boneless chicken thighs
    (about 1¼ pounds), halved
1 small onion, chopped, or ⅓ cup frozen chopped onion
12 ounces button mushrooms, brushed of dirt and thickly sliced
18 baby carrots (about 8 ounces)
20 pitted prunes (about 4 ounces)
2 teaspoons dried thyme
1 teaspoon dried rosemary
½ teaspoon salt
¼ teaspoon freshly ground black pepper
½ cup no-salt, fat-free chicken broth
2 teaspoons whole-wheat flour

1. Heat the oil in a large skillet or high-sided sauté pan set over medium heat. Add the chicken and cook until brown, turning once, about 2 minutes. Transfer to a plate.

2. Add the onion to the pan and cook, stirring, until softened, about 2 minutes. Add sliced mushrooms and continue cooking, stirring occasionally, until they have given off their liquid, about

3 minutes. Add the carrots, prunes, thyme, rosemary, salt, and pepper and cook until fragrant, about 1 minute. Finally, pour in the broth, scraping up any browned bits from the bottom of the pan.

3. Return the chicken and any accumulated juices to the pan. Bring the mixture to a simmer, stir well, cover, and reduce heat to low. Simmer, stirring occasionally, until the chicken is cooked through and the sauce is thickened somewhat, about 25 minutes.

4. Uncover and sprinkle whole-wheat flour over the ingredients. Stir well, then cook just until thickened, about 30 seconds. Serve at once.

# Arroz con Pollo

Translated into English, the name of this dish is chicken with rice. It's a Spanish-inspired casserole made heart-healthy with the inclusion of vegetables and brown rice. Although optional, the saffron gives the dish a characteristic Spanish flavor.

**6 servings**

2 teaspoons olive oil
12 small skinless and boneless chicken thighs
    (about $1\frac{3}{4}$ pounds), halved
1 small onion, chopped, or $\frac{1}{3}$ cup frozen chopped onion
2 garlic cloves, minced
1 ($14\frac{1}{2}$-ounce) can no-salt-added diced tomatoes
$1\frac{1}{2}$ cups water
1 teaspoon dried oregano
1 teaspoon dried thyme
1 teaspoon sweet paprika
$\frac{1}{2}$ teaspoon salt
$\frac{1}{4}$ teaspoon freshly ground black pepper
$\frac{1}{8}$ teaspoon saffron threads, optional
1 bay leaf
1 cup uncooked brown rice
1 cup fresh peas, or 1 cup frozen peas, thawed

1. Preheat oven to 350°F.

2. Heat the oil in a 3-quart Dutch oven or pot set over medium heat. Add the chicken thighs and cook, turning once, until browned, about 2 minutes. Transfer to a plate.

3. Add the onion and garlic and cook, stirring, until softened, about 2 minutes. Pour in the tomatoes and water and stir well to scrape up any browned bits from the bottom of the pot. Add the oregano, thyme, paprika, salt, pepper, saffron (if using), and bay leaf. Bring to a simmer, then stir in brown rice, browned chicken thighs, and any accumulated juices.

4. Cover and bake until the rice is tender, about 1 hour. Sprinkle the peas over the top, cover, and bake 5 more minutes. Stir well, discard the bay leaf, and serve.

# Turkey Vegetable Soup

**NUTRIENT ANALYSIS**

| Calories | 117 |
|---|---|
| Protein | 15 g |
| Carbohydrate | 11 g |
| Total Fat | 2 g |
| Saturated Fat | trace |
| Cholesterol | 28 mg |
| Fiber | 3 g |
| Sugars | 0 g |
| Sodium | 395 mg |

Each serving counts as ½ protein and 1 nonstarchy vegetable.

Soup is one of the ultimate high-response cost foods. Behavioral scientists have long studied it as a bona fide weight-control tool, discovering in numerous experiments that soup reduces hunger and controls caloric intake. Why is this so? Because soup generally takes a long time to eat, prolonging mealtime and thereby allowing your body's natural hunger signals to kick in. What's more, soup makes you feel fuller because it takes up a lot of space in your stomach. You are less likely to want much else (such as dessert), and you will wind up eating a lot less at your meal when soup is on the menu. Here is one of our favorite main-dish soups, prepared with five different vegetables.

*(continued on next page)*

Turkey Vegetable Soup *(cont.)*

**6 servings**

Nonstick spray
1 medium onion, chopped, or ¾ cup frozen chopped onion
4 ribs celery, thinly sliced (about 2 cups)
3 medium carrots, thinly sliced (about 2 cups)
6 ounces mushrooms, brushed of any dirt and thinly sliced
    (about 3 cups)
2 medium tomatoes, seeded and chopped (about ¾ cup)
½ pound cooked turkey breast meat, cut into small chunks
    and slivers
1 teaspoon dried thyme
1 tablespoon dried dill
4 cups no-salt, fat-free chicken broth
½ teaspoon salt

1. Spray a large nonstick saucepan with nonstick spray and set over medium heat. Add the onion, celery, and carrots and cook, stirring, until softened and aromatic, about 3 minutes. Add the mushrooms and tomatoes and cook, stirring occasionally, until the mushrooms have begun to give off their liquid and it is simmering, about 2 minutes.

2. Add the turkey and cook, stirring, just until lightly browned, about 1 minute. Add the thyme and dill and cook 20 seconds. Pour in the broth, scraping up any browned bits from the bottom of the pan. Cover, reduce the heat to low, and simmer 30 minutes, until the vegetables are tender and the soup smells terrific. Season with salt and serve at once.

# Halibut Baked in Packets

| NUTRIENT ANALYSIS | |
| --- | --- |
| Calories | 194 |
| Protein | 32 g |
| Carbohydrate | 8 g |
| Total Fat | 4 g |
| Saturated Fat | .5 g |
| Cholesterol | 46 mg |
| Fiber | 2 g |
| Sugars | 0 g |
| Sodium | 497 mg |

Each serving counts as 1 protein and 1 nonstarchy vegetable.

The very idea that fish does not taste good unless it's fried is ridiculous. Yet many people I've worked with on their weight issues believe this, and they pay a steep price in terms of poor weight control. Please do yourself this favor: Open your eyes to the wide range of possibilities that exist for preparing fish and seafood. Let this recipe, and the others that follow, be your starting point.

Baking fish in packets, as is done here, is perfect for calling the delicate flavors of seafood out of hiding. Afraid of fish bones? Run your fingers carefully over the surface of the fillets to check for bones. Also, these fillets should be skinned for best results; if yours are not, make three diagonal cuts across each fillet's skin, scoring into the flesh without cutting through it.

**4 servings**

4 (5-ounce) skinned halibut fillets, or other white fish fillets such
   as sea bass, red snapper, or tilapia
12 cherry tomatoes, halved
4 artichoke hearts, packed in water, drained, rinsed, and halved
1 yellow squash, diced (about 1 cup)
1 green bell pepper, cored, seeded, and thinly sliced
6 teaspoons freshly squeezed lemon juice
2 tablespoons plus 2 teaspoons chopped fresh dill, or
   2 teaspoons dried
1 teaspoon salt
1/2 teaspoon freshly ground black pepper

1. Preheat oven to 500°F.

*(continued on next page)*

Halibut Baked in Packets *(cont.)*

2. Place each fillet on a 16-inch-long piece of parchment paper or nonstick aluminum foil. Top each fillet with 6 tomato halves, 2 artichoke halves, and ¼ of the squash and bell pepper. Sprinkle 2 teaspoons lemon juice, 2 teaspoons fresh dill or ½ teaspoon dried dill, ¼ teaspoon salt, and ⅛ teaspoon pepper over each. Seal and crimp the packets closed and transfer them to a large, rimmed baking sheet.

3. Bake in the preheated oven for 12 minutes. Transfer to serving plates, let stand 2 or 3 minutes, and serve. (Since the steam is hot, you'll want to open any served to children.)

# Dijon-Roasted Salmon

| NUTRIENT ANALYSIS | |
|---|---|
| Calories | 249 |
| Protein | 26 g |
| Carbohydrate | 2 g |
| Total Fat | 15 g |
| Saturated Fat | 3 g |
| Cholesterol | 72 mg |
| Fiber | trace |
| Sugars | 0 g |
| Sodium | 128 mg |

Each serving counts as 1 protein.

Few types of fish pack more health-protective omega-3 fatty acids than salmon. Two servings a week furnish more than enough of what is now recommended to add health to your life. According to new dietary research, eating more salmon, as well as tuna, mackerel, or cod, may help you program your body to lose pounds by improving your metabolism.

**4 servings**

1 tablespoon whole black peppercorns
1 tablespoon dried dill
¼ teaspoon freshly grated or ground nutmeg (*see* Note)
4 (5-ounce) salmon fillets, checked for bones
2 tablespoons plus 2 teaspoons Dijon mustard
Nonstick spray

1. Preheat oven to 500°F. Place a shallow metal roasting or broiler pan in the oven and let it get very hot as you prepare the salmon.

2. Place the peppercorns in a mortar and grind with the pestle until coarse and cracked. Alternatively, place the peppercorns between two small sheets of wax paper and crack them with a meat mallet or the bottom of a large, heavy saucepan. Pour the cracked peppercorns into a small bowl and combine with the dill and nutmeg.

3. Lay salmon fillets on a clean work surface or a cutting board, skin side down. Coat flesh of each fillet evenly with 2 teaspoons mustard, spreading it all the way to the edges. Sprinkle each fillet with 1/4 of the cracked peppercorn mixture.

4. Using a sturdy oven mitt or pot holder, take the hot roasting pan out of the oven; spray it lightly with nonstick spray. Use a metal spatula to transfer the fillets to the pan, skin side down. Return the pan to the oven and roast until the fillets are cooked through, about 10 minutes. (You can use the point of a knife to separate the meat's filaments slightly to make sure it's opaque, not gelatinous. Do not overcook.) Serve at once.

**NOTE:** Ground nutmeg is more pungent than freshly grated and tends to become rancid rather quickly. Although it takes a little more time, try to grate it fresh if possible.

# Poached Cod with Warm Pineapple Salsa

| NUTRIENT ANALYSIS | |
| --- | --- |
| Calories | 175 |
| Protein | 26 g |
| Carbohydrate | 14 g |
| Total Fat | 1 g |
| Saturated Fat | trace |
| Cholesterol | 62 mg |
| Fiber | 1 g |
| Sugars | trace |
| Sodium | 94 mg |

Each serving counts as 1 protein and approximately 1/2 fruit.

Most fish recipes, like the one here, take very little time and very few cooking skills. Of course, eating more fish is an excellent way to get your weight moving in the right direction, and it may improve the quality of your health. This recipe is poached right in a fruit-based sauce that is naturally sweet, and topped with a quick-fix salsa.

**4 servings**

1 cup unsweetened pineapple juice
1/2 teaspoon cumin seeds
1/4 teaspoon ground cinnamon
1/4 teaspoon crushed red-pepper flakes
1 (1-pound) cod fillet, cut in half
2 tablespoons chopped red onion
1 cup chopped fresh pineapple, or 1 (8-ounce) can pineapple
    chunks in unsweetened juice, drained
2 tablespoons chopped fresh cilantro

1. Place the pineapple juice, cumin seeds, cinnamon, and red-pepper flakes in a 10-inch skillet with a lid and bring to a simmer over medium heat. Reduce heat to low and simmer slowly, uncovered, for 5 minutes.

2. Add the cod, cover the pan, and cook on low for 8 minutes. If you insert a dinner knife into the fillet, hold it there 2 seconds, then gently touch the side of the knife to your lips, it should feel warm. Gently remove the fillets to a serving plate using a large metal spatula. Tent with foil.

3. Add the onion to the sauce, raise heat to high, and boil until reduced to a glaze, about 5 minutes. Stir in the pineapple chunks and cilantro and cook 30 seconds. Pour the sauce over the fillets and serve. Each ½ fillet will make 2 servings.

# Shrimp Teriyaki

**NUTRIENT ANALYSIS**

| | |
|---|---|
| Calories | 162 |
| Protein | 25 g |
| Carbohydrate | 12 g |
| Total Fat | 1 g |
| Saturated Fat | trace |
| Cholesterol | 221 mg |
| Fiber | 2 g |
| Sugars | 2 g |
| Sodium | 400 mg |

Each serving counts as 1 protein, 1 nonstarchy vegetable, and ½ fruit.

Here is a way to prepare shrimp that deserves high-priority status in your meal planning. Low in just about everything except nutrition, this recipe maintains just the right level of necessary sweetness from the teriyaki sauce and pineapple.

**4 servings**

1¼ pounds large shrimp (about 15 shrimp per pound), peeled and deveined
¼ cup bottled teriyaki sauce
8 bamboo skewers
1 green bell pepper, cored, seeded, and cut into 1-inch squares
1 red onion, cut into quarters, then divided into sections about two layers thick
1 cup canned unsweetened pineapple chunks, drained

1. Toss the shrimp and teriyaki sauce in a large bowl. Cover and refrigerate 1 hour, tossing occasionally. At the same time, soak the bamboo skewers in a large glass of water.

2. Preheat broiler.

3. Thread the shrimp, bell pepper sections, onion wedges, and pineapple chunks onto the skewers, dividing the ingredients

(continued on next page)

Shrimp Teriyaki *(cont.)*

evenly among the skewers. Wrap the ends of the skewers in small pieces of aluminum foil to keep them from burning. Lay them in the broiler pan or in a shallow metal roasting pan. (Lining the pan with nonstick aluminum foil makes cleanup a snap later on.)

4. Broil 5 inches from the heat until the shrimp begin to turn pink, about 2 minutes. Turn and continue broiling just until the shrimp are pink and firm, about 2 more minutes. Serve at once.

# Crab Chowder

| NUTRIENT ANALYSIS | |
| --- | --- |
| Calories | 180 |
| Protein | 16 g |
| Carbohydrate | 22 g |
| Total Fat | 3 g |
| Saturated Fat | trace |
| Cholesterol | 46 mg |
| Fiber | 2 g |
| Sugars | 0 g |
| Sodium | 389 mg |

Each serving counts as ½ protein, 1 nonstarchy vegetable, ½ starchy carbohydrate, and approximately ⅓ low-fat dairy product.

This is absolutely the best—and creamiest—crab chowder I have ever tasted, and you would never know it was prepared without cream. Fat-free evaporated milk and a small grated potato substitute for the cream and do the job of thickening just as effectively, but without the saturated fat. It is a great way to create something healthier for yourself, your family, and your guests.

**6 servings**

2 teaspoons canola oil
1 medium onion, chopped, or ³/4 cup frozen chopped onion
3 ribs celery, thinly sliced
1¹/2 cups frozen corn kernels, thawed
1 teaspoon dried thyme
¹/2 teaspoon salt
¹/4 teaspoon freshly ground black pepper
2 cups no-salt, fat-free vegetable broth

1 cup fat-free evaporated milk
1 bay leaf
1 small baking potato (4 ounces), peeled
¾ pound lump crabmeat, picked over for shell and cartilage
¼ cup chopped fresh cilantro
3–4 dashes Tabasco sauce, optional

1. Heat the oil in a large saucepan set over medium heat. Add the onion and celery and cook, stirring, until softened, about 3 minutes. Stir in the corn, then the thyme, salt, and pepper and cook 20 seconds, until fragrant. Pour in the vegetable broth and evaporated milk and add the bay leaf. Stir well, then cover and simmer 5 minutes.

2. Using the smallest holes of a box grater or an old-fashioned potato grater, grate the potato into the chowder. Stir well, cover again, and simmer another 5 minutes, until slightly thickened.

3. Add the crab and cilantro and cook until crab is just heated through, about 1 minute. Stir in the Tabasco, if desired. Serve at once.

# Three Bean Chili

**NUTRIENT ANALYSIS**

| | |
|---|---|
| Calories | 172 |
| Protein | 8 g |
| Carbohydrate | 34 g |
| Total Fat | 3 g |
| Saturated Fat | trace |
| Cholesterol | 0 mg |
| Fiber | 8 g |
| Sugars | 2 g |
| Sodium | 660 mg |

Each serving counts as
1 vegetarian protein (or 1 starchy
carbohydrate) and 1 nonstarchy
vegetable.

The official state dish of Texas is chili. This version, however, is not traditional Texas-style chili because, in Texas, chili has no beans. This recipe is the absolute reverse: all beans, no meat. Nor is it as screaming hot as most Texas chili, which you have to stash in the refrigerator to keep from burning down the house. The three varieties of beans in this chili make it a high-yield vegetarian dish, loaded with fiber (naturally beneficial for lifetime weight control), B vitamins, potassium, magnesium, phosphorus, and zinc. If you prefer to use only one kind of bean, three cups of red kidney beans work best. Draining and rinsing canned beans removes most of their sodium content, thus eliminating unneeded extra salt.

**6 servings**

2 teaspoons olive oil
1 large onion, chopped, or 1¼ cups frozen chopped onion
2 ribs celery, thinly sliced
1 large green bell pepper, cored, seeded, and chopped
2 garlic cloves, minced
2 tablespoons chili powder
2 teaspoons ground cumin
1 (14½-ounce) can no-salt-added diced tomatoes
1 cup canned great Northern beans, drained and rinsed
1 cup canned pinto beans, drained and rinsed
1 cup canned red kidney beans, drained and rinsed
2 cups no-salt, fat-free vegetable broth
1 medium sweet potato, peeled
½ teaspoon salt

1. Heat oil in a large saucepan or pot set over medium heat. Add the onion, celery, and green pepper. Cook, stirring, until fragrant, about 3 minutes. Add the garlic and cook 30 seconds, then stir in the chili powder and cumin. Cook another 20 seconds, until aromatic.

2. Pour in the tomatoes, beans, and broth and bring to a simmer.

3. Using the large holes of a box grater, grate the sweet potato into the chili. Cover, reduce heat to low, and simmer slowly, stirring occasionally, until thickened, about 40 minutes. Stir in the salt and let stand at room temperature for 5 minutes before serving.

# Mac and Cheese

**NUTRIENT ANALYSIS**

| | |
|---|---|
| Calories | 183 |
| Protein | 18 g |
| Carbohydrate | 27 g |
| Total Fat | trace |
| Saturated Fat | trace |
| Cholesterol | 10 mg |
| Fiber | 2 g |
| Sugars | 0 g |
| Sodium | 443 mg |

Each serving counts as
1 low-fat dairy product, 1 starchy
carbohydrate, and 1 nonstarchy
vegetable.

Sure to please every member of your family, this is a lighter, healthier update of a family favorite, one that is just as rich and creamy as its traditional counterpart, but without the excess calories and saturated fat. It's made with whole-wheat pasta, a high-response, high-yield carbohydrate that, unlike white pasta, has not been stripped of its nutritional value. The artichoke hearts add not only fiber but also extra richness (make sure you select those packed in water, not in oil).

## 6 servings

Nonstick spray
2 cups fat-free milk
1 tablespoon whole-wheat flour
6 ounces shredded fat-free mozzarella cheese
$1^1/_2$ teaspoons onion powder
$^1/_2$ teaspoon garlic powder
$^1/_2$ teaspoon sweet paprika
$^1/_2$ teaspoon salt
$^1/_4$ teaspoon grated nutmeg
$^1/_4$ teaspoon freshly ground black pepper
8 canned artichoke hearts, packed in water, drained, rinsed, and
      roughly chopped
3 cups cooked whole-wheat elbow macaroni

1. Preheat oven to 350°F. Spray a $1^1/_2$ quart high-sided, round baking or soufflé dish with nonstick spray and set aside.

2. Heat the milk in a large saucepan set over medium-low heat. When small bubbles appear around the edge of the pan, whisk in the whole-wheat flour. Continue cooking and whisking until

thickened, about 20 seconds. Stir in cheese and cook, stirring, until it melts and the mixture is smooth.

3. Stir in the onion powder, garlic powder, paprika, salt, nutmeg, and pepper; then stir in the artichoke hearts and macaroni. Cook just until heated through, about 30 seconds.

4. Mound the mixture into the prepared baking dish and press down lightly to compact. Bake until bubbling and lightly browned, about 20 minutes. Let stand 5 minutes before serving.

# Curried Lentil Stew

**NUTRIENT ANALYSIS**

| | |
|---|---:|
| Calories | 212 |
| Protein | 15 g |
| Carbohydrate | 39 g |
| Total Fat | 1 g |
| Saturated Fat | trace |
| Cholesterol | 0 mg |
| Fiber | 17 g |
| Sugars | 0 g |
| Sodium | 208 mg |

Each serving counts as 1 vegetarian protein (or 1 starchy carbohydrate) and 1 nonstarchy vegetable. The amount of fruit in this recipe is negligible.

This full-bodied vegetarian entrée has as its focus lentils, which are about as nutrient dense a food as you will find. Lentils are a rich source of natural iron and fiber and contain virtually no fat, thus packing maximum nutrition into every portion. Further enhancing the nutritional value of this meal is a string of high-response cost, high-yield foods: apples and various vegetables, including napa cabbage (Chinese cabbage), which is known for its bounty of vitamin C.

## 8 servings

2 teaspoons curry powder (*see* Note)
4 cups no-salt, fat-free vegetable broth
2 cups dried green lentils, rinsed
1 large onion, chopped, or 1¼ cups frozen chopped onion
2 parsnips, peeled and chopped (1 cup)
2 tart apples such as Granny Smith, peeled, cored, and roughly chopped
5 cups shredded napa cabbage
1 teaspoon salt
½ teaspoon freshly ground black pepper

1. Heat the curry powder in a large saucepan or pot set over medium heat until fragrant, about 10 seconds. Pour in the vegetable broth, then stir in the lentils, onion, parsnips, and apples. Bring to a simmer.

2. Lay the shredded cabbage on top of the simmering stew. Cover the pot, reduce heat to low, and simmer 10 minutes, undisturbed.

3. Sprinkle the salt and pepper over the top and stir the stew to incorporate the steamed cabbage. Cover again and simmer, stirring occasionally, until the lentils are tender and the stew is slightly thickened, about 30 minutes.

4. Scoop out 1 cup of the stew and place it in a food processor fitted with the chopping blade or a large blender. Process or blend until smooth. Stir the puree back into the stew and cook about 1 minute, just until heated through. Serve at once.

**NOTE:** Curry powder is actually a blend of spices, not an individual spice. Thus, there are hundreds of varieties on the market. You can use the standard yellow curry powder found in the spice rack of most grocery stores (it's yellow from turmeric), but you can also search out other products, some of them quite fiery, at gourmet and Indian markets.

# Enchiladas with Barbecued Greens

**NUTRIENT ANALYSIS**

| | |
|---|---|
| Calories | 154 |
| Protein | 9 g |
| Carbohydrate | 18 |
| Total Fat | 4.5 g |
| Saturated Fat | 1 g |
| Cholesterol | 6 mg |
| Fiber | 2 g |
| Sugars | 3 g |
| Sodium | 439 mg |

Each serving counts as 1 starchy carbohydrate, 1 nonstarchy vegetable, and 1 low-fat dairy product.

Enchiladas are an icon of Tex-Mex cooking, a cuisine deeply rooted in the combined cultures of Texas and Mexico. This recipe recasts traditional enchiladas as a delicious vegetarian entrée with the unusual addition of Swiss chard, a leafy plant so high yielding in vitamins and minerals that it has been deemed worthy of growing on planetary space stations. In addition, by making your own barbecue sauce you avoid low-response cost, low-yield corn syrup and sweeteners found in most commercial brands.

**4 servings**

2 teaspoons canola oil
1 medium onion, chopped, or ¾ cup frozen chopped onion
2 garlic cloves, minced
3 tablespoons unsweetened frozen apple-juice concentrate, thawed
1 tablespoon tomato paste
1 tablespoon raisins
1 teaspoon liquid smoke (*see* Note)
½ teaspoon ground cumin
½ teaspoon dried oregano
½ teaspoon salt
¼ teaspoon freshly ground black pepper
2–3 dashes Tabasco sauce
1 pound Swiss chard, stemmed, leaves washed but not dried and roughly chopped (4 cups packed greens)
4 large corn tortillas
4 ounces packaged low-fat shredded Mexican cheese blend

1. Preheat oven to 350°F.

2. Heat the oil in a large saucepan set over medium heat. Add the onion and cook, stirring, until softened, about 2 minutes. Add the garlic and cook 30 seconds.

3. Stir in the apple-juice concentrate and tomato paste and cook, stirring, until the tomato paste dissolves. Reduce heat to low, then stir in the raisins, liquid smoke, cumin, oregano, salt, pepper, and Tabasco.

4. Stir in the greens, cover the pan, and simmer until they're wilted, about 3 minutes. Stir well, cover, and set aside off the heat for 5 minutes to blend the flavors.

5. Lay one tortilla on a clean, dry work surface or cutting board. Scoop about $1/2$ cup filling into the center of the tortilla, then roll closed. Transfer the rolled tortilla to a baking dish just large enough to hold all four stuffed enchiladas securely. Repeat with the other tortillas and remainder of the filling. Sprinkle cheese over the enchiladas, covering them completely.

6. Bake until cheese and filling are bubbling, about 20 minutes. Let stand at room temperature 5 minutes before serving.

NOTE: There are many brands of liquid smoke on the market. Look for a bottle that contains nothing but smoke distillate (mesquite or hickory works best in this recipe) and water, no chemical additives or fillers.

# Spaghetti Squash with Mushroom Marinara Sauce

**NUTRIENT ANALYSIS**

| | |
|---|---|
| Calories | 156 |
| Protein | 4 g |
| Carbohydrate | 26 g |
| Total Fat | 5 g |
| Saturated Fat | 1 g |
| Cholesterol | 0 mg |
| Fiber | 3 g |
| Sugars | 0 g |
| Sodium | 527 mg |

Each serving counts as
1 nonstarchy vegetable.

If you are accustomed to large plates of pasta, but don't like the weight gain associated with such supersized portions, substituting spaghetti squash—comprised of pastalike strands you can twirl around your fork—is a workable strategy. Spaghetti squash is a perfect stand-in for high-carb white pasta, and it mingles well with other ingredients, including this fast-prep mushroom marinara sauce.

**6 servings**

1 (4-pound) spaghetti squash
2 ounces dried mushrooms, preferably shiitake or porcini
1 cup boiling water
1 (26-ounce) jar marinara sauce (3 cups)

1. Preheat oven to 350°F.

2. Prick the spaghetti squash four or five times with a fork, place it on a rimmed baking sheet, and bake for 1½ hours until soft.

3. Meanwhile, place the dried mushrooms in a medium bowl and cover them with the boiling water. Set aside to soften for about 15 minutes.

4. Drain the mushrooms, reserving liquid they soaked in. If liquid is sandy, pass it through a colander lined with cheesecloth or two sheets of paper towels to strain it.

5. Chop the mushrooms, discarding tough stems. Place them and the strained liquid in a medium saucepan set over medium heat.

Bring to a simmer, then reduce heat to low and cook until the liquid has reduced by half, about 5 minutes. Stir in the marinara sauce and cook until heated through, about 2 minutes. Cover and set aside to keep warm.

6. Once the squash is soft, cool 10 minutes at room temperature. Cut squash in half; scrape out and discard the seeds. Use a fork to shred pulp into its natural threads, letting them fall into a large bowl. (You should have about 6 cups of squash threads.) Add the sauce, toss well, and serve.

# Zucchini Lasagna

| NUTRIENT ANALYSIS | |
| --- | --- |
| Calories | 317 |
| Protein | 32 g |
| Carbohydrate | 14 g |
| Total Fat | 15 g |
| Saturated Fat | 5 g |
| Cholesterol | 65 mg |
| Fiber | 3 g |
| Sugars | 7 g |
| Sodium | 823 mg |

Each serving counts as ½ protein, 1 nonstarchy vegetable, and 1 low-fat dairy product.

If you are Italian, or simply a fan of Italian cuisine, losing weight does not mean you have to abandon your culture or your love of food. It does, however, require that you make a few minor substitutions in order to offset the effects of fat-promoting refined carbohydrates in your diet. As a positive step in this direction, try this taste-good, noodleless zucchini lasagna, which is calorie- and carb-controlled to help you manage your weight.

**8 servings**

3 large zucchini, washed but not peeled
2 teaspoons salt, or less, as needed
2 teaspoons olive oil
4 garlic cloves, minced
1 teaspoon fennel seeds
¼ teaspoon crushed red-pepper flakes
1 pound lean ground beef
1 (26-ounce) jar marinara sauce (3 cups)
Nonstick spray
1½ cups fat-free ricotta
4 ounces shredded fat-free mozzarella
¼ cup pasteurized egg substitute
1 teaspoon freshly grated or ground nutmeg (*see* Note, page 129)
1 tablespoon whole-wheat bread crumbs
2 tablespoons freshly grated Parmesan cheese

1. Use a cheese plane to slice the zucchini into long strips. To do this, hold the vegetable in one hand, then pull the plane down it, creating a long strip about ¼-inch thick. Clean and dry your work surface and line it with paper towels. Lay zucchini strips on the

paper towels in a single layer; sprinkle both sides lightly with salt, and let stand at room temperature for 15 minutes, turning strips once as they sweat out their moisture.

2. Meanwhile, heat the oil in a large saucepan set over medium heat. Add the garlic and cook, stirring, until lightly browned, about 30 seconds. Add the fennel seeds and red-pepper flakes and cook 30 seconds. Crumble in the ground beef and continue cooking and stirring until the meat is browned, about 3 minutes. Stir in the marinara sauce, bring to a simmer, cover, and reduce the heat to low. Simmer about 10 minutes.

3. Preheat oven to 350°F. Spray a 9 x 13–inch baking dish with nonstick spray.

4. Thoroughly combine the ricotta, mozzarella, egg substitute, and nutmeg in a large bowl and set aside.

5. Use fresh paper towels to wipe salt and moisture from the zucchini strips. Gently squeeze the strips between fresh paper towels to remove any excess moisture, but take care not to crush or tear them.

6. Build the lasagna by sprinkling the bottom of the prepared baking dish with 1 teaspoon whole-wheat bread crumbs. Lay 1/3 of the zucchini slices in the bottom of the pan, overlapping as necessary. Spoon 1/3 of the red sauce over them, then spread 1/2 the cheese mixture over the sauce. Sprinkle with 1 teaspoon bread crumbs, then layer with 1/2 the remaining zucchini slices. Spoon 1/2 the remaining sauce over them, then spread the rest of the cheese mixture over the top. Sprinkle with remaining 1 teaspoon bread crumbs. Finish with remaining zucchini sauce. Sprinkle with grated Parmesan.

7. Bake until bubbling and quite hot, about 50 minutes. Let stand 5 minutes before slicing and serving.

# Carrots Alfredo

| NUTRIENT ANALYSIS | |
| --- | --- |
| Calories | 96 |
| Protein | 6 g |
| Carbohydrate | 14 g |
| Total Fat | 2 g |
| Saturated Fat | trace |
| Cholesterol | 2 mg |
| Fiber | 4 g |
| Sugars | trace |
| Sodium | 69 mg |

Each serving counts as
1 vegetarian protein,
1 nonstarchy vegetable, and
less than 1/4 low-fat dairy
product.

If you haven't already, try making tofu a part of the way you cook. It is a versatile vegetarian food that takes on the flavor of the food with which it is paired and supplies a wealth of protein with very little fat and almost no cholesterol. In this recipe, silken soft tofu, which has a rather custardlike consistency, is used to create a dairy-free pasta sauce served over beta-carotene–rich carrots.

**4 servings**

1 pound carrots, peeled
1 pound silken soft tofu (about ³/₄ cup)
²/₃ cup low-fat milk or soy milk
¹/₂ teaspoon freshly grated or ground nutmeg
   (*see* Note, page 129)
¹/₄ teaspoon freshly ground black pepper
¹/₂ teaspoon freshly grated Parmesan cheese

1. Bring a large pot of water to a boil over high heat. Use a vegetable peeler to make long carrot strips, much like flat noodles, pulling the peeler along the length of the carrot and letting the strips fall into a bowl. (There will be some waste, some small inner core of the carrot you can't peel into strips—reserve these pieces in the refrigerator for a snack another day.) You should have about 4 cups of packed carrot strips.

2. Drop the strips into the boiling water and boil 1 minute. Drain and rinse under cool water. Set aside.

3. Place the tofu and milk or soy milk in a food processor fitted with the chopping blade and process until smooth, scraping down

the sides of the bowl as necessary. Pour the puree into a 10-inch nonstick skillet set over medium heat and bring to a simmer. Stir in the nutmeg and pepper. Remove the pan from heat and stir in the Parmesan and carrot strips. Toss well before serving.

# Asian Tofu Stew

| NUTRIENT ANALYSIS | |
| --- | --- |
| Calories | 153 |
| Protein | 9 g |
| Carbohydrate | 25 g |
| Total Fat | 3 g |
| Saturated Fat | trace |
| Cholesterol | 0 mg |
| Fiber | 3 g |
| Sugars | 3 g |
| Sodium | 473 mg |

Each serving counts as
1 vegetarian protein and
1 nonstarchy vegetable.

If you are a vegetarian, or even if you're not, introduce something brand new into your standard repertoire of meals with this modern variation on an ancient Chinese method of stewing in soy sauce, vinegar, and broth. Tofu contains beneficial plant chemicals technically known as isoflavones, which have been proved to help lower blood cholesterol levels.

**4 servings**

4 scallions, trimmed and minced
2 carrots, peeled and minced
2 garlic cloves, minced
1 cup no-salt, fat-free vegetable broth
3 tablespoons reduced-sodium soy sauce
2 tablespoons peeled and minced fresh ginger
    (*see* Note, page 101)
2 tablespoons rice vinegar or white wine vinegar
12 ounces silken firm tofu, cut into $1/2$-inch cubes
    (about 2 cups)
16 shiitake mushrooms, stems discarded, caps quartered
2 tablespoons cornstarch whisked with 1 tablespoon water

(continued on next page)

Asian Tofu Stew *(cont.)*

1. Place the scallions, carrots, garlic, broth, soy sauce, ginger, and vinegar in a large saucepan set over medium-high heat. Cover, bring to a boil, then reduce heat and simmer slowly for 5 minutes to blend the flavors and cook the carrots.

2. Add the tofu cubes and mushrooms, cover again, and continue simmering 10 minutes. Stir occasionally but very gently, taking care not to break up the tofu.

3. Raise heat to medium-high. Pour in the cornstarch mixture, stir gently, and cook just until thickened, about 20 seconds. Remove from heat, cover, and let stand 5 minutes before serving.

# Silver-Dollar Steak Fries

### NUTRIENT ANALYSIS

| | |
|---|---|
| Calories | 97 |
| Protein | 3 g |
| Carbohydrate | 22 g |
| Total Fat | trace |
| Saturated Fat | 0 g |
| Cholesterol | 0 mg |
| Fiber | 2 g |
| Sugars | 0 g |
| Sodium | 357 mg |

Each serving counts as 1 starchy carbohydrate.

This is my very favorite low-fat side dish—a method of fixing potatoes that is surely the path to your partner's heart in more ways than one, since it is prepared in a heart-healthy manner. The recipe forgoes the buckets of oil or lard usually used for deep frying and replaces all that fat with vegetable spray, which contains only 1 or 2 calories per spray.

**4 servings**

Nonstick spray
4 medium baking potatoes, preferably russet
2 tablespoons commercial barbecue dry rub
1 teaspoon salt

1. Position the racks in the top and bottom thirds of the oven; preheat to 425°F. Spray two rimmed baking sheets with the non-stick spray.

2. Slice potatoes into ¼-inch-thick medallions and place them on prepared baking sheets. Lightly spray the potatoes with the non-stick spray. Sprinkle the slices lightly with the barbecue dry rub and salt.

3. Bake 30 minutes, then reverse the sheets top to bottom and continue baking until the medallions are browned, about 30 more minutes, 40 minutes for very crisp.

For toppings, try one of the following: ½ cup fat-free sour cream mixed with 2 tablespoons finely chopped chives or the green parts of scallions, ½ cup ketchup mixed with 1 teaspoon jarred horseradish and 1 teaspoon freshly squeezed lemon juice, or ½ cup fat-free yogurt mixed with 1 tablespoon Dijon mustard and 2 teaspoons curry powder.

# Winter Root Vegetable Puree

**NUTRIENT ANALYSIS**

| | |
|---|---:|
| Calories | 77 |
| Protein | 2 g |
| Carbohydrate | 18 g |
| Total Fat | trace |
| Saturated Fat | 0 g |
| Cholesterol | 0 mg |
| Fiber | 4 g |
| Sugars | 0 g |
| Sodium | 309 mg |

Each serving counts as
1 nonstarchy vegetable.
The vegetables in this recipe
contain some starch, but it is
minimal.

When you make the decision to get your weight and your health under control, you must stop moving in the direction you're going and make a nutritional U-turn that will help you become the fit, vibrant person you really want to be. This means stepping out and trying some new foods and some new ways of preparing them. Here's one way to start, with a delicious reduced-carbohydrate alternative to mashed potatoes. This puree not only tastes good, it is filled with disease-fighting vitamins, minerals, and fiber. You can use a food processor to make a smoother puree, but a standard mixer will do the trick, too.

**8 servings**

3 parsnips (about ⅔ pound), peeled and cut in 1-inch slices
1 medium rutabaga (about 1 pound), peeled and cut in
    1-inch cubes
1 large turnip (about ¾ pound), peeled and cut in 1-inch cubes
⅓ cup no-salt, fat-free vegetable broth
2 tablespoons fat-free sour cream
1½ teaspoons Dijon mustard
½ teaspoon salt
¼ teaspoon freshly ground black pepper
1 scallion, minced, optional

1. Place the parsnips, rutabaga, and turnip in a large saucepan. Add water to cover and bring to a boil over high heat. Cover, reduce the heat to low, and simmer until vegetables are tender when pierced with a fork, about 20 minutes. Drain.

2. Place the cooked vegetables, broth, sour cream, mustard, salt, and pepper in a food processor fitted with the chopping blade. Pulse twice to combine ingredients, then process until smooth,

scraping down the sides of the bowl as necessary, about 30 seconds. If desired, garnish with scallion just before serving.

# Ratatouille

| NUTRIENT ANALYSIS | |
|---|---|
| Calories | 86 |
| Protein | 3 g |
| Carbohydrate | 16 g |
| Total Fat | 2 g |
| Saturated Fat | trace |
| Cholesterol | 0 mg |
| Fiber | 5 g |
| Sugars | 0 g |
| Sodium | 184 mg |

Each serving counts as
1 nonstarchy vegetable.

Not eating at least five servings of fruits and vegetables a day may make you feel so physically imbalanced that you fail to operate at peak levels. Here's a solution: ratatouille, a bonanza of vegetables prepared in a delicious, highly nutritious stew. Low-calorie ratatouille is another excellent example of a high-response cost, high-yield dish because it takes time to eat and is filling. Vegetables and olive oil are true hunger suppressors—foods that help control appetite and make you feel more satisfied after eating a meal that contains them.

**6 servings**

2 teaspoons olive oil
1 large onion, thinly sliced
4 garlic cloves, minced
8 Roma tomatoes, chopped
2 large zucchini, halved lengthwise and cut into $1/4$-inch slices
1 medium eggplant, cut into $3/4$-inch cubes
1 green bell pepper, cored, seeded, and thinly sliced
2 teaspoons dried thyme
1 teaspoon dried rosemary
1 tablespoon capers, drained and rinsed, optional
$1/2$ teaspoon salt
$1/4$ teaspoon freshly ground black pepper

*(continued on next page)*

Ratatouille *(cont.)*

1. Heat the oil in a large saucepan set over medium heat. Add the onion and cook, stirring, until softened, about 3 minutes. Add the garlic and cook until fragrant, about 30 seconds.

2. Add the tomatoes, zucchini, eggplant, bell pepper, thyme, and rosemary and stir until tomatoes break down and the juice begins to simmer, about 4 minutes. Cover and reduce heat to low. Simmer, stirring occasionally, until the vegetables have softened and formed a stew, about 35 minutes.

3. Uncover, stir in the capers, if using, and simmer until the mixture thickens slightly, about 10 more minutes. Season with salt and pepper just before serving.

# Black-Eyed Peas and Greens

**NUTRIENT ANALYSIS**

| | |
|---|---|
| Calories | 95 |
| Protein | 7 g |
| Carbohydrate | 14 g |
| Total Fat | 3 g |
| Saturated Fat | .5 g |
| Cholesterol | 10 mg |
| Fiber | 4 g |
| Sugars | 0 g |
| Sodium | 938 mg |

Each serving counts as 1 starchy carbohydrate and 1 nonstarchy vegetable.

Although I feel that luck comes only to those who have planned carefully for it, many people eat for luck, particularly at the beginning of each new year as a part of a New Year's Day tradition. A very popular dish is Hoppin' John, a Southern dish traditionally made with black-eyed peas and bacon. This version scales down the fat and pumps up the nutrition by including turkey bacon and Swiss chard. Who knows? Perhaps this lucky dish will bring you good fortune on your journey toward weight loss!

**4 servings**

4 strips turkey bacon, roughly chopped
3 garlic cloves, minced
1½ cups canned black-eyed peas, drained and rinsed
1 pound Swiss chard, stemmed, leaves washed but not dried and roughly chopped (4 cups packed greens)
⅓ cup no-salt, fat-free vegetable broth
½ teaspoon salt
2 to 3 dashes Tabasco sauce, optional

1. Heat a large saucepan over medium heat. Add the bacon and cook, stirring often, until browned, about 2 minutes. Add the garlic and cook until fragrant, about 20 seconds. Stir in the black-eyed peas and cook 30 seconds, stirring constantly.

2. Lay the chard on top of the beans and pour in the broth. Cover the pan, reduce heat to low, and simmer until the chard is wilted, about 3 minutes. Stir in the salt and Tabasco, if using, mixing the wilted greens into the black-eyed peas. Serve at once.

# Radish Slaw

| NUTRIENT ANALYSIS | |
| --- | --- |
| Calories | 37 |
| Protein | 1 g |
| Carbohydrate | 7.5 g |
| Total Fat | trace |
| Saturated Fat | 0 g |
| Cholesterol | 0 mg |
| Fiber | 2 g |
| Sugars | 1 g |
| Sodium | 259 mg |

Each serving counts as
1 nonstarchy vegetable.

Isn't there some way to escape the same-old, same-old salads that turn up on just about every diet plan? Glad you asked! Here is a spectacular, slenderizing slaw prepared with three high-response cost, high-yield vegetables that provide an appetite-controlling benefit together with incredible flavor. This recipe makes enough for a crowd.

**12 servings**

3/4 cup fat-free mayonnaise
1 tablespoon Dijon mustard
1 tablespoon apple-cider vinegar
2 teaspoons celery seed
2 teaspoons dried dill
1 teaspoon salt
1/2 teaspoon freshly ground black pepper
20 large radishes, shredded (about 4 cups)
2 red or green bell peppers, cored and seeded, then shredded
    (about 2 cups)
1 small cabbage, cored, outer leaves removed, then shredded
    (about 2 cups, packed)

1. Whisk the mayonnaise, mustard, vinegar, celery seed, dill, salt, and pepper in a small bowl until creamy; set aside.

2. Toss the shredded radishes, bell peppers, and cabbage in a large bowl. Add the dressing and stir until the vegetables are well coated. For the best flavor, cover and refrigerate 30 minutes before serving, then stir to reincorporate any accumulated liquid.

# Roasted Beets

**NUTRIENT ANALYSIS**

| | |
|---|---|
| Calories | 123 |
| Protein | 3 g |
| Carbohydrate | 13 g |
| Total Fat | 8 g |
| Saturated Fat | 1 g |
| Cholesterol | 0 mg |
| Fiber | 4 g |
| Sugars | 0 g |
| Sodium | 298 mg |

Each serving counts as
1 nonstarchy vegetable and 1 fat.
The fruit portion is negligible and
is included for taste.

Promise yourself that you will try at least one new vegetable per week for the next month. Expand your food repertoire—just to prove you can do it. This week, why not start with beets? Their deep-red color comes from a purple pigment with antioxidant powers possibly strong enough to help shield you against cancer and heart disease. When you buy beets for this recipe, do not discard the greens. See Wilted Beet Greens (page 156) for a nutritious way to create a bed of greens for your roasted beets. (Tip: Lemon juice will remove the red stains on your hands that result from preparing beets.)

**6 servings**

¼ cup walnut pieces
2 pounds beets (about 6 medium), peeled and cut into
    ½-inch cubes
2 tablespoons walnut oil or olive oil
1 teaspoon salt
½ teaspoon freshly ground black pepper
2 tablespoons balsamic vinegar
1 cup water-packed mandarin orange sections, drained
2 scallions, thinly sliced
2 teaspoons chopped fresh rosemary

1. Preheat oven to 400°F.

2. Place the walnuts on a rimmed baking sheet and toast them in the oven until lightly browned, about 5 minutes. Set aside.

3. Place the beets in a shallow roasting pan or a broiler pan. Add the oil, salt, and pepper and toss well. Bake, tossing occa-

*(continued on next page)*

Roasted Beets *(cont.)*

sionally, until beets are tender when pierced with a fork, about 40 minutes.

4. Remove the pan from the oven and pour in the vinegar. Stir gently but thoroughly, scraping up any browned bits from the bottom of the pan while taking care not to mash the beets. Transfer the mixture to a large bowl and cool 5 minutes.

5. Stir in the mandarin orange sections, walnut pieces, scallions, and rosemary. Serve warm, at room temperature, or cold.

# Wilted Beet Greens

**NUTRIENT ANALYSIS**

| | |
|---|---|
| Calories | 8 |
| Protein | 1 g |
| Carbohydrate | 2 g |
| Total Fat | 0 g |
| Saturated Fat | 0 g |
| Cholesterol | 0 mg |
| Fiber | 1.5 g |
| Sugars | 0 g |
| Sodium | 193 mg |

Each serving counts as 1 nonstarchy vegetable.

Remove the tough red stems running down the center of the leaves, then chop the leaves. Rinse the leaves under cold running water and put in a large nonstick skillet with just the water clinging to the leaves. Set over medium-high heat, cover, reduce the heat to low, and steam until wilted and tender, about 5 minutes. Season the greens with $1/2$ teaspoon salt before serving.

# Asparagus with a Warm Vinaigrette

| NUTRIENT ANALYSIS | |
| --- | --- |
| Calories | 29 |
| Protein | 2 g |
| Carbohydrate | 5 g |
| Total Fat | trace |
| Saturated Fat | 0 g |
| Cholesterol | 0 mg |
| Fiber | 2 g |
| Sugars | 0 g |
| Sodium | 272 mg |

Each serving counts as
1 nonstarchy vegetable.

Wake up to the fact that vegetables are among your best nutritional bargains. On the food plans outlined for you in *The Ultimate Weight Solution Food Guide,* nonstarchy vegetables such as asparagus are a category of food you can eat to your heart's content, so don't shortchange yourself. In the recipe below, one serving of asparagus (6 spears) provides more than one-third of your day's need for a crucial B vitamin called folate. You can use the same recipe for green beans; just remember to snip the ends.

**4 servings**

24 fresh asparagus spears, tough bottoms trimmed, spears
    cut into thirds
¼ cup fat-free Italian salad dressing (*see* Note)
1 tablespoon chopped fresh flat-leaf parsley leaves
2 teaspoons chopped fresh oregano leaves
1 teaspoon chopped fresh thyme leaves
¼ teaspoon freshly ground black pepper
2 tablespoons sliced almonds, optional

1. Place the asparagus in a large skillet, cover with water, and bring to a simmer over high heat. Cook until crisp-tender, no more than 2 minutes. Drain in a colander, then refresh under cold running water.

2. Return the skillet to medium heat, add the dressing, and stir until warmed, about 30 seconds. Return the asparagus to the pan and toss well with the dressing. Stir in the parsley, oregano,

*(continued on next page)*

Asparagus with a Warm Vinaigrette *(cont.)*

thyme, pepper, and almonds, if using. Heat 10 seconds before serving.

**NOTE:** Although it's not fat-free, you can make a tasty home-made vinaigrette with nut oil. Whisk 2 tablespoons of walnut or almond oil, 1 tablespoon of white-wine vinegar, and $1/2$ teaspoon salt in a small bowl, then pour the mixture into the skillet to warm.

# Glazed Squash

| NUTRIENT ANALYSIS | |
| --- | --- |
| Calories | 116 |
| Protein | 2 g |
| Carbohydrate | 30 g |
| Total Fat | trace |
| Saturated Fat | 0 g |
| Cholesterol | 0 mg |
| Fiber | 3 g |
| Sugars | 0 g |
| Sodium | 183 mg |

Each serving counts as 1 starchy carbohydrate and $1/4$ fruit.

A create-your-own-experience approach to living most definitely applies to your health. You're accountable for the choices you make, right down to what you eat every single day of your life. When you choose healthy, you choose the experience of better health. One category of food to put on your healthy-choice list is winter squash, a champion health builder. Squash is filled with nutrients like vitamin C and beta carotene, both of which strengthen your immune system. One of the best-tasting varieties of winter squash is acorn squash, which is naturally sweet and endowed with a generous fund of fiber. When prepared simply, as in this recipe, it makes a delicious complement to virtually any meat, fish, or poultry main dish.

**4 servings**

2 medium acorn squash, peeled, halved, seeded, and cut into
    $1/2$-inch cubes (*see* Note)
1 cup unsweetened apple juice
1 (4-inch) stick cinnamon
4 allspice berries
$1/2$ teaspoon salt
$1/4$ teaspoon freshly grated or ground nutmeg
    (*see* Note page 129)

1. Place the cubed squash in a large saucepan and add the apple juice. Add the cinnamon stick and allspice berries, place saucepan over high heat, and bring to a boil. Cover, reduce heat to low, and simmer until the squash is tender when pierced with a fork, about 12 minutes.

2. Use a slotted spoon to transfer the squash to a serving bowl; cover and set aside. Remove and discard the cinnamon stick and allspice berries.

3. Increase heat to medium-high and boil the liquid until it has thickened and reduced to a glaze, about 3 minutes. You should have about 2 tablespoons of glaze. Stir in salt and nutmeg, pour the glaze over the cooked squash, and serve at once.

**NOTE:** You can also use 1 large butternut squash, 2 medium kabochee squash, or 1 medium blue hubbard squash.

# Snacks

Through healthy snacking, you can take a huge step toward changing and, ultimately, controlling your weight for a lifetime. Eating three meals per day, with the right kind of snacks in between, helps keep your blood sugar levels even throughout the day, so that your brain doesn't signal a pressing need for extra food, and you have less desire to overeat. What's more, a series of meals, including at least two snacks, paced throughout the day also keeps your metabolism running in high gear. So, snacking on high-response cost, high-yield foods is actually critical to your weight-control success.

By contrast, snacking on low-response cost, low-yield foods such as chips, cookies, snack cakes, or other such items can add up to hundreds and hundreds of unneeded calories a day, plus the resultant weight gain.

The purpose of a healthy snack is also to supplement your diet with extra nutrients. Accordingly, the snacks in this chapter have been designed to give you good nutritional value. Each one is delicious and filling, and the result is a collection of snacks that are not only good for you but also destined to become the ones you and your family enjoy most.

# Sun-dried Tomato Spread

| NUTRIENT ANALYSIS | |
| --- | --- |
| Calories | 56 |
| Protein | 6 g |
| Carbohydrate | 8 g |
| Total Fat | trace |
| Saturated Fat | trace |
| Cholesterol | 5 mg |
| Fiber | 2 g |
| Sugars | 0 g |
| Sodium | 525 mg |

Each serving counts as
1 nonstarchy vegetable.

This fat-free snack calls for sun-dried tomatoes, which give the spread its tangy flavor. Spread the mixture into celery ribs for a crunchy, high-response cost, high-yield snack.

**8 servings**

8 ounces fat-free cream cheese, cubed
2 garlic cloves
1 cup soft and pliable sun-dried tomatoes (*see* Note)
2 tablespoons freshly squeezed lemon juice
1 teaspoon dried basil
1 teaspoon dried oregano
1 teaspoon fennel seed
$^1/_2$ teaspoon salt
$^1/_4$ teaspoon freshly ground pepper
16 celery ribs

1. Place the cream cheese, garlic, sun-dried tomatoes, lemon juice, basil, oregano, fennel, salt, and pepper in a food processor fitted with the chopping blade. Pulse three times, then process until smooth, about 1 minute. If necessary, stop the processor occasionally to scrape down the sides of the bowl.

2. Spread 2 tablespoons of the mixture into each celery rib; cut them into thirds and serve at once. Or, store the spread, tightly covered, in the refrigerator for up to 2 days; allow it to come back to room temperature before using.

**NOTE:** Sun-dried tomatoes should be very soft, not wooden and desiccated. For best results, look for them sealed in shrink wrap in the produce section or loose at Italian markets. In all cases, test them to make sure they are pliable. If not, place in a large bowl, cover with boiling water, and let stand 1 minute, then drain and blot dry. Do not use sun-dried tomatoes packed in oil.

# Seasoned Popcorn

In America, we eat more popcorn than any other snack, munching nearly 17 billion quarts annually, or 59 quarts for every man, woman, and child in the country. Although healthy, low in fat, and high in fiber, this irresistible snack is usually drenched in butter or oil, making it an off-limits snack if your goal is weight loss. There are, however, any number of ways to fix popcorn without buttering or oiling it. For a change of pace, give your popcorn a new spin with these three easy seasonings. You might really be surprised by the outcome. Be sure to use air-popped popcorn and add the spices while it is hot.

| NUTRIENT ANALYSIS | |
| --- | --- |
| Calories | 71 |
| Protein | 2 g |
| Carbohydrate | 14 g |
| Total Fat | 1 g |
| Saturated Fat | 0 g |
| Cholesterol | 0 mg |
| Fiber | 3 g |
| Sugars | 0 g |
| Sodium | 352 mg |

Each serving counts as 1 starchy carbohydrate.

## Barbecue Popcorn

### 4 servings

1 tablespoon mild paprika
1 teaspoon hickory-smoked salt (*see* Note)
1 teaspoon onion powder
1/2 teaspoon ground cumin
1/2 teaspoon garlic powder
8 cups air-popped popcorn
Nonstick butter-flavored spray, such as I Can't Believe It's Not Butter

*(continued on next page)*

Seasoned Popcorn (*cont.*)

Combine the paprika, hickory-smoked salt, onion powder, cumin, and garlic powder in a small bowl. Spread the warm popcorn on a large, rimmed baking sheet and spray lightly with nonstick spray. Sprinkle the spice mixture over popcorn, toss, and serve at once.

**NOTE:** Hickory-smoked salt is available in some supermarkets and gourmet food shops, as well as by mail order on the Internet.

| NUTRIENT ANALYSIS | |
|---|---|
| Calories | 84 |
| Protein | 4 g |
| Carbohydrate | 14 g |
| Total Fat | 3 g |
| Saturated Fat | 1 g |
| Cholesterol | 4 mg |
| Fiber | 2.5 g |
| Sugars | 0 g |
| Sodium | 271 mg |

Each serving counts as 1 starchy carbohydrate.

# Parmesan Popcorn

### 4 servings

$1/4$ cup grated low-fat Parmesan cheese
1 tablespoon dried parsley flakes
2 teaspoons dried oregano
2 teaspoons dried basil
$1/2$ teaspoon garlic salt
8 cups air-popped popcorn

Combine the Parmesan, parsley, oregano, basil, and garlic salt in a small bowl. Spread the warm popcorn on a large, rimmed baking sheet and sprinkle the spice mixture over it. Toss well and serve at once.

**NUTRIENT ANALYSIS**

| | |
|---|---|
| Calories | 76 |
| Protein | 2 g |
| Carbohydrate | 14 g |
| Total Fat | 1 g |
| Saturated Fat | trace |
| Cholesterol | 0 mg |
| Fiber | 3 g |
| Sugars | 0 |
| Sodium | 292 mg |

Each serving counts as 1 starchy carbohydrate.

# Spicy Orange Popcorn

## 4 servings

2 tablespoons dried orange peel, ground (*see* Note)
2 teaspoons ground allspice
1 teaspoon dry mustard
1 teaspoon freshly grated or ground nutmeg (*see* Note page 129)
1 teaspoon ground ginger
1/2 teaspoon salt
1/4 teaspoon cayenne pepper, optional
8 cups air-popped popcorn
Nonstick butter-flavored spray, such as I Can't Believe It's Not Butter

Combine grated orange peel, ground allspice, dry mustard, nutmeg, ginger, salt, and cayenne pepper, if using, in a small bowl. Spread the warm popcorn on a large, rimmed baking sheet and spray it lightly with nonstick spray. Sprinkle the spice mixture over the popcorn, toss, and serve at once.

**NOTE:** Dried orange and lemon peel are available in the spice section of most supermarkets; the ground powder is less readily available. To make your own, grind twice the amount of dried peel called for in the recipe in a small food processor, a clean coffee grinder, or a spice grinder. Or crush it in a mortar with a pestle. Remeasure the powder to be sure you have the correct amount.

# Miniature Cracker Pizzas

Attention all pizza lovers: With these imaginative minipizzas, which use whole-grain crackers as their base, you'll have great pizza taste without the calories and refined carbs that usually go with it. They are also perfect for a party appetizer tray.

**4 servings**

1 teaspoon dried oregano
1 teaspoon dried basil
1/4 teaspoon crushed red-pepper flakes, optional
16 low-salt Triscuit crackers
16 soft and pliable sun-dried tomatoes (*see* Note page 162)
5 tablespoons plus 1 teaspoon shredded fat-free provolone or
    mozzarella cheese

1. Preheat broiler. Combine oregano, basil, and red-pepper flakes, if using, in a small bowl and set aside.

2. Place the crackers on a rimmed baking sheet, lay a sun-dried tomato on each one, and top with 1 teaspoon cheese.

3. Place about 5 inches below the heat source and broil just until the cheese melts, about 15 seconds. Sprinkle the herb mixture over the minipizzas and serve at once.

# Asian Chickpea Dip

**NUTRIENT ANALYSIS**

| | |
|---|---|
| Calories | 136 |
| Protein | 5 g |
| Carbohydrate | 18 g |
| Total Fat | 5 g |
| Saturated Fat | trace |
| Cholesterol | 0 mg |
| Fiber | trace |
| Sugars | 0 mg |
| Sodium | 253 mg |

Each serving counts as approximately 1 starchy carbohydrate or 1 vegetarian protein.

If you want to see less of yourself in the coming months, try experimenting with new, more slenderizing ways to prepare dips. The key is to substitute low-fat and fat-free ingredients for standard ingredients, such as sour cream. The pureed beans featured in this recipe are among the easiest and most wholesome stand-ins you can find. Add wasabi (made from a Japanese variety of horseradish) to spice up the beans, and serve with raw carrots and celery.

**4 servings**

1 (15-ounce) can chickpeas (garbanzo beans),
    drained and rinsed
1 garlic clove, cut in three pieces
¼ cup water
2 tablespoons freshly squeezed lemon juice
1 tablespoon sesame oil
1 tablespoon reduced-sodium soy sauce
1 teaspoon wasabi paste, or 2 teaspoons wasabi powder mixed
    with 2 teaspoons water

Place the chickpeas, garlic, water, lemon juice, sesame oil, soy sauce, and wasabi paste in a food processor fitted with the chopping blade. Pulse two or three times to combine, scrape down the sides of the bowl, then process until smooth, about 1 minute. Transfer mixture to serving bowl and serve at room temperature, or store it in the refrigerator, tightly covered, up to 2 days.

**NOTE:** This dip can be made in a blender, but you will have to stop the motor and use a narrow rubber spatula or the handle of

*(continued on next page)*

Asian Chickpea Dip *(cont.)*

a wooden spoon to push the ingredients down onto the blades several times during the process. The resulting dip will be thicker than that made in the food processor. If it's too thick, add up to 2 more tablespoons water.

# Guacamole

| NUTRIENT ANALYSIS | |
|---|---|
| Calories | 75 |
| Protein | 3 g |
| Carbohydrate | 5 g |
| Total Fat | 5.5 g |
| Saturated Fat | 1 g |
| Cholesterol | 0 mg |
| Fiber | 2 g |
| Sugars | trace |
| Sodium | 226 |

Each serving counts as
1 nonstarchy vegetable and 1 fat
and yields a negligible amount of
vegetarian protein.

Among south-of-the-border dips, guacamole usually wins the popularity contest hands down. Along with potassium and a slew of vitamins, avocados are filled with monounsaturated fats, which help lower LDL (or bad) cholesterol and triglycerides while raising HDL (or good) cholesterol. This recipe calls for light silken tofu to give the mixture a creamy texture as well as an extra dose of protein. Serve with raw, cut-up vegetables.

**6 servings**

6 ounces light silken tofu ($^3$/4 cup)
1 ripe Haas avocado, pitted and peeled (*see* Note)
1 large tomato, finely chopped
$^1$/4 cup minced red onion
2 tablespoons freshly squeezed lemon juice
2 tablespoons packed fresh cilantro, chopped
$^3$/4 teaspoon salt
$^1$/2 teaspoon ground cumin
3–5 dashes Tabasco sauce

1. Place the tofu and avocado in a medium bowl and mash with a fork until creamy.

2. Stir in the tomato, red onion, lemon juice, cilantro, salt, cumin, and Tabasco. Serve at once or cover and refrigerate up to 2 hours.

**NOTE:** In markets you will generally find two varieties of avocado, the lighter green, smoother type from Florida, and the darker, pebbly skinned Haas variety, which is smaller and creamier than the Florida avocado.

# Fruit Dip

| NUTRIENT ANALYSIS | |
|---|---|
| Calories | 12 |
| Protein | 0 g |
| Carbohydrate | 9 g |
| Total Fat | trace |
| Saturated Fat | trace |
| Cholesterol | 0 mg |
| Fiber | 2 g |
| Sugars | 0 g |
| Sodium | 2 mg |

Each serving counts as 1 free food.

Here is an unusual, imaginative, and tasty snack idea: a dry dip for dried fruit, fresh apple or pear slices, or fresh strawberries. Prepare the dip in bulk and store it in a tightly covered jar in a cool, dark part of your pantry to have on hand whenever you want a special treat.

**8 servings**

Granulated sugar substitute to equal 1/4 cup sugar
  (see product label)
3 tablespoons ground cinnamon
2 tablespoons ground dried lemon or orange peel
  (*see* Note, page 165)
1 teaspoon ground allspice
1 teaspoon ground cloves
1/2 teaspoon freshly grated or ground nutmeg (*see* Note, page 129)

Combine all the ingredients in a small bowl and store, tightly covered, up to 2 months. (One serving is a heaping tablespoon.)

# Stuffed Dates

| NUTRIENT ANALYSIS | |
|---|---:|
| Calories | 189 |
| Protein | 6 g |
| Carbohydrate | 38 g |
| Total Fat | 2 g |
| Saturated Fat | trace |
| Cholesterol | 5 mg |
| Fiber | 4 g |
| Sugars | trace |
| Sodium | 171 mg |

Each serving counts as 1 fruit and approximately 1 fat.

Dates are rich in fiber, B vitamins, potassium, magnesium, and iron. For this recipe, look for large, plump, pitted dates such as the Medjool variety, which work best for stuffing. This recipe can be doubled or tripled for parties.

**4 servings**

4 ounces fat-free cream cheese, softened
1/4 cup sugar-free orange marmalade or all-fruit spread
20 large pitted dates
20 sliced almonds (about 3 tablespoons)

1. Using a fork or wooden spoon, combine the cream cheese and marmalade in a small bowl until creamy.

2. Using a paring knife, make a slit along the long side of each date and gently pry open without splitting it. Divide the cream cheese mixture evenly among the dates, spooning it into the slit and mounding it up slightly, using a scant 2 teaspoons per date.

3. Top each with a sliced almond and serve.

# Raspberry Lemonade

## NUTRIENT ANALYSIS

| | |
|---|---|
| Calories | 72 |
| Protein | 1 g |
| Carbohydrate | 19 g |
| Total Fat | 0 g |
| Saturated Fat | 0 g |
| Cholesterol | 0 mg |
| Fiber | 2 g |
| Sugars | 6 g |
| Sodium | 2 mg |

Each serving counts as 1 fruit.

For a new twist on lemonade, try this summer thirst quencher made with antioxidant-rich raspberries.

**6 servings**

2 pints fresh raspberries, or 1 (12-ounce) bag frozen
　　raspberries, thawed
4 cups water
2 cups lemon juice, freshly squeezed or unsweetened purchased
1/2 cup unsweetened white grape–juice concentrate, thawed
Granulated sugar substitute to equal 1/2 cup sugar
　　(see package label)

Use the back of a wooden spoon to press the raspberries through a fine-mesh sieve placed over a large pitcher to strain out the seeds. Add the water, lemon juice, grape-juice concentrate, and sugar substitute and stir well. (Alternatively, place all the ingredients in a large blender and blend until fairly smooth, then strain the mixture into a large pitcher through a fine-mesh sieve or a colander lined with a double layer of paper towels to remove the raspberry seeds.) In either case, serve over ice or cover and store in the refrigerator up to 4 days.

# Desserts

# 7

People, by nature, want what they can't have, and, on most so-called diets, you can't have many types of desserts. What I want you to recognize is that when you or someone else, or even a diet, tells you that you can't have certain foods, you can expect that your desire for them will intensify. Because you're feeling sorry for yourself, you may overeat or binge in order to compensate for your sense of deprivation and, as a result, you'll blow your food plan. To achieve and maintain a desirable weight, however, does not mean you have to turn down or forgo desserts. With just a few minor substitutions for sugar and fat, and a little creativity, you can prepare and enjoy desserts that will help slim you down and give you the results you are looking for.

The wonderful thing about this chapter is that it features desserts that are not only more healthful than regular sweets but also filling, with the ability to tame your cravings for more sweet stuff. As high-response cost, high-yield desserts, they will satisfy you in a big way, so you won't find yourself reaching for another slice or piece of something that would sabotage your weight-control efforts.

These are not fattening, nutrition-poor foods. They depend on the natural sweetness of fruit and low-calorie flavorings for their great taste and appetizing appeal, and they all include protein, calcium, and other essential nutrients.

So, if you like desserts, you have come to the right place. Indulge yourself, and enjoy!

# Apricot Cheesecake

When you want cheesecake, but not the calories, sugar, and fat that usually comes with it, here is your solution: a very dense cheesecake with a creamy texture that will satisfy your taste without disrupting your weight-management efforts.

**8 servings**

4 cups fat-free plain yogurt
6 ounces dried apricot halves, preferably tart California variety
2 cups boiling water
Nonstick spray
1 cup Great Grains Crunchy Pecans cereal
1/3 cup frozen unsweetened apple-juice concentrate, thawed
6 ounces fat-free cream cheese, cut in chunks and softened
2 large eggs, at room temperature (*see* Note 1)
1 large egg white, at room temperature
Granulated sugar substitute equivalent to 3 tablespoons sugar
    (see package label)
1 tablespoon vanilla extract
1/2 teaspoon salt (*see* Note 2)

1. Line a colander or sieve with damp paper towels and place over a large bowl. Spoon the yogurt into colander and set it aside to drain for about 3 hours, or until 1 1/2 cups of liquid have drained from the yogurt.

2. Meanwhile, place the apricots in a medium bowl and cover with the boiling water. Let stand until softened, about 30 minutes. Drain and set aside.

3. Position a rack in the center of the oven and preheat to 350°F.

4. Spray the inside of an 8-inch springform pan (*see* Note 3) with nonstick spray. Place the cereal in a food processor fitted with the chopping blade and process until finely ground, about 30 seconds. Alternatively, place the cereal in a zipper plastic bag, squeeze out all the air, and seal tightly. Using a heavy rolling pin or the bottom of a large, heavy saucepan, pulverize the cereal to the texture of fine meal, rotating the bag frequently so all cereal is crushed. Pour the ground cereal into the sprayed springform pan. Rotate and tip the pan until the cereal coats the bottom and sides to form a crust.

5. Place the softened apricots and apple-juice concentrate in a food processor fitted with the chopping blade or in a large blender and process or blend until fairly smooth, about 1 minute. (If using a blender, you may need to stop it often to scrape it down with a rubber spatula or the handle of a wooden spoon.)

6. Add the cream cheese, eggs, egg white, sugar substitute, vanilla, and salt to the food processor or blender and process or blend until quite smooth, about 1 minute. Gently pour the mixture into the prepared springform pan, taking care not to disturb the crust.

7. Bake until firm and set but still a little jiggly, like a custard, about 1 hour. Place on a wire rack and cool to room temperature, about 1 hour. Cover tightly and refrigerate in the pan for at least 2 hours before serving.

8. To serve, release the latch on the pan and gently unmold the cake. Because the cake is moist, do not remove the pan bottom. Set the cake, still on pan bottom, on a serving platter for slicing. Cheesecake can be stored in the refrigerator, covered, up to 3 days.

**NOTE 1:** For the most part, eggs need to be at room temperature when making desserts. Cold eggs can shock batters and pre-

*(continued on next page)*

Apricot Cheesecake *(cont.)*

vent baked goods from rising to their full height. To bring eggs to room temperature, let them stand for 15 minutes, or place them in a large bowl of warm (not hot) water for 3 minutes before using.

**NOTE 2:** Salt is the secret ingredient pastry chefs use to make desserts sparkle. It heightens sweetness, particularly in fruit desserts. You can omit it if you prefer, but the final dish will have slightly less pizzazz.

**NOTE 3:** A springform pan is a high-sided baking pan with removable sides and bottom, available in almost all houseware stores. A latch releases the sides of the pan so that you can remove the cake without turning the pan upside down and perhaps damaging the delicate baked product.

# Banana Cream Pie

| NUTRIENT ANALYSIS | |
| --- | --- |
| Calories | 233 |
| Protein | 9.5 g |
| Carbohydrate | 37 g |
| Total Fat | 5 g |
| Saturated Fat | trace |
| Cholesterol | 2.5 mg |
| Fiber | 2 g |
| Sugars | 4 g |
| Sodium | 510 mg |

Each serving counts as
¼ fruit, ½ starchy carbohydrate,
½ low-fat dairy product, and
trace of fat.

Banana cream pie is always a treat and a favorite at family get-togethers. If you are among the banana cream pie lovers of the world, you'll surely enjoy what's in store for you here. The fat and calories have been cut back, but with no corresponding loss of richness or flavor. And, there's an unexpected nutritional bonus: a healthy dose of fiber and lots of calcium in every bite.

**8 servings**

2½ cups Banana Nut Crunch Cereal
2 tablespoons light margarine spread, at room temperature

2 (1-ounce) packages sugar-free, fat-free instant banana cream
    or vanilla pudding mix
2 tablespoons fat-free powdered dry milk
2 cups cold fat-free milk
2 ripe bananas, peeled and roughly chopped
2 cups sugar-free, fat-free vanilla yogurt

1. Position a rack in the lower third of the oven and preheat to 325°F.

2. Place the cereal in a food processor fitted with the chopping blade and process until finely ground, about 30 seconds. Add the margarine spread and process until a soft ball of dough begins to form. Pour the dough into a 9-inch pie pan and press it into an even crust across the bottom and up the sides of the pan. Alternatively, place the cereal in a zipper plastic bag, squeeze out all the air, and seal tightly. Using a heavy rolling pin or the bottom of a large, heavy saucepan, pulverize the cereal to the texture of fine meal, rotating the bag frequently so the cereal is uniformly crushed. Transfer the cereal to a medium bowl and cut in the margarine spread with a pastry cutter or two forks, until the mixture begins to form a dough. Press the dough into the pie pan as indicated.

3. Bake for 10 minutes, then transfer to a wire rack and cool completely, about 30 minutes.

4. Place the pudding mix and powdered dry milk in a large bowl. Pour in the milk and whisk 1 minute. Add the chopped bananas and continue whisking until somewhat thickened, about 1 more minute. Pour into the prepared pie shell and refrigerate until set, about 2 hours. Pie may be stored in the refrigerator, tightly covered, up to 3 days.

5. Just before serving, spread the yogurt evenly over the pie, forming a creamy topping.

# Sweet Potato Pie

| NUTRIENT ANALYSIS | |
| --- | --- |
| Calories | 208 |
| Protein | 7 g |
| Carbohydrate | 43 g |
| Total Fat | 2 g |
| Saturated Fat | trace |
| Cholesterol | 54 mg |
| Fiber | 4 g |
| Sugars | 3.5 g |
| Sodium | 449 mg |

Each serving counts as
1 starchy carbohydrate. There
is a negligible amount of protein
and low-fat dairy in each serving
as well.

If you recall my nutritional assessment in *The Ultimate Weight Solution,* I ask the question: "During the week, how many servings of orange or yellow vegetables or fruit do you eat?" Answering "three or more" would be a good indicator that you are getting ample vitamin A and other protective nutrients from orange and yellow fruits and vegetables. If your score shows anything less, you're skimping here and need to jack up your nutrition. One way to accomplish that is by serving up the following Southern favorite—a delicious sweet potato pie that gives you plenty of nutrition and plenty of flavor.

**8 servings**

3 medium sweet potatoes (about 8 ounces each)
2 cups Grape-Nuts cereal
1/2 cup sugar-free maple syrup
2 large eggs, at room temperature
1/2 cup fat-free evaporated milk
Granulated sugar substitute equivalent to 2 tablespoons sugar
    (see product label)
Granulated brown sugar substitute equivalent to 2 tablespoons
    sugar (*see* Note 1)
1/2 teaspoon ground ginger
1/2 teaspoon ground cinnamon
1/2 teaspoon salt

1. Position a rack in the center of the oven and preheat to 400°F.

2. Place the sweet potatoes on rimmed baking sheet (see Note 2) and bake until soft, about 1 hour. Set aside to cool for 20 minutes. Reduce oven temperature to 350°F.

3. Combine the Grape-Nuts and maple syrup in a medium bowl. Press the mixture into a 9-inch pie pan, forming an even crust along the bottom and sides but not over the rim—any crust that is not touching the filling may burn during baking.

4. Cut the cooled sweet potatoes in half and scoop the soft flesh into a large bowl. (You should have 2 cups mashed flesh; reserve any leftovers in the refrigerator for another use.) Whisk in the eggs, evaporated milk, granulated sugar substitutes, ginger, cinnamon, and salt, until smooth. Gently pour the mixture into the prepared pie pan, taking care not to disturb the crust.

5. Bake until firm and set, about 45 minutes. Cool on a wire rack at least 30 minutes before serving. (A few cracks may appear on the surface while cooling.) Once completely cooled, the pie may be stored, uncovered, at room temperature up to 12 hours, or it may be refrigerated, tightly covered, up to 3 days.

**NOTE 1:** Granulated brown sugar substitute is available in the baking aisle of most supermarkets. If you can't find it, just use a regular granulated sugar substitute (for a total equivalent to 3 tablespoons sugar in the recipe).

**NOTE 2:** Sweet potatoes need to be placed on a sheet to catch any drips from the caramelized juices that leak out while baking. If you line the baking sheet with aluminum foil, cleanup will be a snap.

# Grasshopper Pie

**NUTRIENT ANALYSIS**

| | |
|---|---:|
| Calories | 242 |
| Protein | 13 g |
| Carbohydrate | 46 g |
| Total Fat | 1 g |
| Saturated Fat | trace |
| Cholesterol | trace |
| Fiber | 3 g |
| Sugars | 6 g |
| Sodium | 492 mg |

Each serving counts as approximately ½ starchy carbohydrate, ¼ vegetarian protein, and ¼ low-fat dairy product.

Few desserts are richer or more elegant than grasshopper pie, another Southern favorite. With a few simple recipe adjustments, this version is greatly streamlined from the original, so that you can enjoy yourself and still stay the course for achieving your weight-management goals.

**8 servings**

2 cups Grape-Nuts cereal
½ cup sugar-free chocolate syrup
1 (12.3-ounce) package silken extra-firm light tofu, cut into cubes
4 tablespoons fat-free powdered dry milk
2½ cups fat-free milk
½ teaspoon mint or peppermint extract
3 drops green food coloring
1 (1-ounce) package sugar-free, fat-free instant vanilla pudding mix
1 (1.4-ounce) package sugar-free, fat-free instant chocolate pudding mix

1. Position a rack in the center of the oven and preheat to 350°F.

2. Combine the cereal and chocolate syrup in a large bowl and press the mixture into a 10-inch pie pan, forming an even crust covering the bottom and sides but not over the rim of the pan. Bake for 10 minutes. Transfer to a wire rack; use the back of a wooden spoon to press the crust against the pie pan, and cool completely, about 1 hour.

3. Place $1/2$ the tofu (about $6^1/8$ ounces), 2 tablespoons powdered dry milk, $1^1/4$ cups fat-free milk, mint extract, and green food coloring in a large blender or a food processor fitted with the chopping blade. Blend or process until smooth, about 30 seconds. Add the vanilla pudding mix and blend or process until slightly thickened, about 20 seconds, then pour into the baked pie shell. Clean and dry the blender or food processor container and blades.

4. Place the remaining tofu, the remaining 2 tablespoons powdered dry milk, and the remaining $1^1/4$ cups milk in the blender or food processor and blend or process until smooth, about 30 seconds. Add the chocolate pudding mix and blend or process for 20 seconds. Gently spread this mixture over the green pudding mixture to form a second layer of filling.

5. Refrigerate until set, about 2 hours. Pie can be stored in the refrigerator, tightly covered, up to 2 days. Serve chilled.

# Vanilla-and-Orange Parfaits

**NUTRIENT ANALYSIS**

| | |
|---|---|
| Calories | 200 |
| Protein | 11 g |
| Carbohydrate | 38 g |
| Total Fat | 1 g |
| Saturated Fat | 0 g |
| Cholesterol | trace |
| Fiber | 1 g |
| Sugars | 6 g |
| Sodium | 465 mg |

Each serving counts as 1 fruit, ¼ low-fat dairy product, and a negligible amount of vegetarian protein.

If, when you were a kid, you liked vanilla ice cream covered with orange sherbet and served on a stick, you'll love its comeback here as a low-fat, sugar-free parfait. Protein-rich tofu easily takes the place of cream to create a dessert that is light but also very filling.

**4 servings**

1 (.3-ounce) package sugar-free orange gelatin
1 cup boiling water
1 cup orange juice
½ (12.3-ounce) package silken firm light tofu
    (about 6⅛ ounces)
1¼ cups fat-free milk
2 tablespoons fat-free powdered dry milk
1 (1-ounce) package fat-free, sugar-free instant vanilla
    pudding mix
1 teaspoon vanilla extract
2 (11-ounce) cans mandarin orange sections packed in
    juice, drained

1. Place the gelatin in a medium bowl and stir in the boiling water until dissolved. Stir in the orange juice, then pour the mixture into an 8-inch-square baking pan. Refrigerate until firm, about 4 hours.

2. Meanwhile, place the tofu, milk, and powdered dry milk in a blender or a food processor fitted with the chopping blade. Blend or process until smooth, about 30 seconds. Add the pudding mix and vanilla and blend or process until somewhat thickened, about 20 seconds. Pour the mixture into a large bowl and refrigerate until firm, about 2 hours.

3. Cut the firm gelatin into 1-inch squares. Place 8 squares in the bottom of four parfait glasses or large footed water glasses. Top each with ¼ cup pudding, then 3 tablespoons of orange sections. Repeat with 8 additional squares gelatin and ¼ cup pudding. Top with the remaining orange sections. Serve at once or cover and refrigerate up to 2 days.

# Cherry Vanilla Parfaits

Here is an easy-to-prepare dessert that looks as good as it tastes. Perfect for guests or family, these parfaits are light and filling, so you won't overdo when it comes time for dessert.

**8 servings**

1 (12.3-ounce) package silken extra-firm light tofu
3 cups fat-free milk
⅓ cup fat-free powdered dry milk
1 teaspoon vanilla extract
2 (1-ounce) packages sugar-free, fat-free instant vanilla
    pudding mix
½ teaspoon salt
1 (20-ounce) can sugar-free cherry pie filling

| NUTRIENT ANALYSIS | |
| --- | --- |
| Calories | 139 |
| Protein | 7 g |
| Carbohydrate | 26 g |
| Total Fat | 1 g |
| Saturated Fat | trace |
| Cholesterol | 2 mg |
| Fiber | trace |
| Sugars | 0 g |
| Sodium | 553 mg |

Each serving counts as ½ low-fat dairy product and 1 fruit. There is a negligible amount of vegetarian protein in this recipe.

1. Place the tofu, milk, powdered dry milk, and vanilla in a blender or a food processor fitted with the chopping blade, and blend or process until smooth, about 30 seconds. Add the pudding mix and salt, scrape down the sides of the container, and blend or process until somewhat thickened, about 20 seconds. Transfer the mixture to a bowl and refrigerate 1 hour.

*(continued on next page)*

Cherry Vanilla Parfaits *(cont.)*

2. Layer the pudding and the cherry pie filling in 8 parfait glasses, beginning with a layer of pudding (2 to 3 tablespoons), followed by a layer of pie filling (about 1 tablespoon), and continuing until you have 3 layers of each. Cover the glasses with plastic wrap and chill for at least 1 hour, or up to 2 days.

# Mocha Fudge Pudding

| NUTRIENT ANALYSIS | |
|---|---|
| Calories | 157 |
| Protein | 14 g |
| Carbohydrate | 23 g |
| Total Fat | 1 g |
| Saturated Fat | 0 |
| Cholesterol | 1 mg |
| Fiber | .5 g |
| Sugars | 0 g |
| Sodium | 420 mg |

Each serving counts as approximately ¼ vegetarian protein and ¼ low-fat dairy product.

This rich and creamy dessert not only satisfies your chocolate cravings but also offers a number of nutritional perks, from high-response cost, high-yield protein in the tofu to bone-building, fat-burning calcium in the milk. The splash of instant coffee actually amplifies its chocolate flavor.

**4 servings**

½ (12.3-ounce) package silken extra-firm light tofu
    (about 6⅛ ounces)
2 cups fat-free milk
¼ cup fat-free powdered dry milk
1 tablespoon instant espresso or coffee powder (*see* Note)
1 (1.4-ounce) package sugar-free, fat-free instant chocolate
    pudding mix
Non-fat, sugar-free vanilla frozen yogurt, optional
Fresh fruit, such as cherries, strawberries, or raspberries,
    optional

1. Place the tofu, milk, powdered dry milk, and instant coffee in a blender or a food processor fitted with the chopping blade and blend or process until smooth and creamy, about 30 seconds. Add the pudding mix and blend or process until somewhat thickened, about 20 seconds.

2. Transfer the mixture to four 1-cup ramekins or serving cups and refrigerate at least 2 hours before serving. The pudding can be made in advance and kept, tightly covered, in the refrigerator, up to 3 days.

3. If you'd like to "gild the lily," you can top the puddings with a dollop of non-fat, sugar-free vanilla yogurt and garnish them with fresh fruit, such as cherries, strawberries, or raspberries.

**NOTE:** Instant espresso powder is found in the beverage or coffee aisles of many supermarkets. For best flavor, store it in the freezer after it's been opened. If you use instant coffee in this recipe, make sure it's a powdered variety, or that it dissolves completely in the milk before you add the pudding mix.

# Pumpkin Custard

| NUTRIENT ANALYSIS | |
| --- | --- |
| Calories | 107 |
| Protein | 6 g |
| Carbohydrate | 15 g |
| Total Fat | 2 g |
| Saturated Fat | 1 g |
| Cholesterol | 6 mg |
| Fiber | 0 g |
| Sugars | 0 g |
| Sodium | 208 mg |

Each serving counts as
approximately ¼ starchy
carbohydrate and ½ low-fat
dairy product. There is a
negligible amount of protein
from the egg substitute in
this recipe.

When you need to prepare a dessert that will please your family and friends during the holidays, consider this convenient, make-ahead custard deliciously flavored with maple and spices. A single serving provides more than half your daily requirement for vitamin A.

## 6 servings

1½ cups solid-packed canned pumpkin (*not* pumpkin pie filling)
1 cup fat-free evaporated milk
¾ cup pasteurized egg substitute
½ cup sugar-free maple syrup
Granulated sugar substitute equivalent to ¼ cup sugar (see product label)
2 tablespoons fat-free powdered dry milk
2 teaspoons vanilla extract
1 teaspoon pumpkin pie spice

1. Position a rack in the center of the oven and preheat the oven to 350°F.

2. Combine all the ingredients in a large bowl and whisk until smooth and creamy. Divide the mixture equally among 6 oven-safe, 1-cup ramekins.

3. Place the filled ramekins on a baking sheet and bake until puffed and set, about 35 minutes. (The custards will still jiggle a little when shaken.) Cool on a wire rack at least 15 minutes before serving. The custards can be stored, covered, in the refrigerator up to 2 days.

# Baked Bananas

Here is a fruit dessert so simple that it can be baking in the oven while you're eating your dinner, so save room for it. The natural sweetness of the bananas makes it taste like a splurge, but, of course, it is anything but. For an added treat, serve the bananas with sugar-free, fat-free vanilla frozen yogurt or ice milk.

**4 servings**

4 (12-inch) pieces aluminum foil
4 large ripe bananas, peeled, split lengthwise, then halved
$1/4$ cup apricot all-fruit spread
1 teaspoon vanilla extract
1 teaspoon rum extract, optional
$1/2$ teaspoon ground cinnamon
$1/2$ teaspoon salt

1. Position a rack in the center of the oven and preheat the oven to 500°F.

2. Lay the pieces of aluminum foil on a work surface, place one quartered banana on each piece, and top with 1 tablespoon fruit spread, $1/4$ teaspoon vanilla and rum extracts (if using), $1/8$ teaspoon cinnamon, and $1/8$ teaspoon salt. Seal the packets and transfer them to a large, rimmed baking sheet.

3. Bake until soft, about 10 minutes. Place the packets on 4 serving plates and let stand, sealed, at room temperature for 3 minutes before serving. Make sure you help any children open their packets because the escaping steam can be very hot.

# Poached Pears

| NUTRIENT ANALYSIS | |
|---|---|
| Calories | 175 |
| Protein | trace |
| Carbohydrate | 44 g |
| Total Fat | 0 g |
| Saturated Fat | 0 g |
| Cholesterol | 0 mg |
| Fiber | 4 g |
| Sugars | 19 g |
| Sodium | 10 mg |

Each serving counts as 2 fruits.

Among fruits, pears offer one of the highest fiber bargains you can find. This is important, since fiber is a weight-control ally that stabilizes your blood sugar and promotes feelings of fullness so that you're less likely to overeat. With more fiber in your diet, you will be on your way to a fitter, healthier body. This recipe borrows from a classic French bistro dessert spiced with cloves and cinnamon for a refreshing flavor.

## 4 servings

4 firm pears, peeled and cored (*see* Note)
1 (15-ounce) can frozen unsweetened white grape–juice
    concentrate, thawed
4 whole cloves
1 (4-inch) cinnamon stick

1. Combine all the ingredients in a large saucepan, add enough water to cover the pears, and bring to a boil over medium-high heat. Cover with parchment or foil and weight with a plate or pan lid to prevent pears from floating. Reduce the heat to low, and simmer until the pears are tender when pierced with the tip of a knife, about 30 minutes.

2. Use a slotted spoon to transfer the pears to a large bowl. Raise the heat under the pan to medium-high and boil the syrup until it's reduced by $2/3$ and somewhat thickened, about 12 minutes. Remove the cloves and cinnamon stick. Pour the syrup over the pears and refrigerate at least 2 hours.

3. Serve each pear with 2 tablespoons of the syrup. Tightly covered, the pears and syrup can be stored in the refrigerator up to 3 days.

**NOTE:** Peeling pears presents no problem, except that it must be done just before you cook them or they will start to turn brown. Coring them is another matter. The best way is to use a melon baller and begin scraping up from the *blossom end,* that is, the wide bottom of the pear, where the desiccated remains of the blossom are sometimes still visible. Scoop up into the flesh with the melon baller, turning as you go, thereby creating a round hole and taking out some of the seeds. Continue coring the pear by turning the melon baller in the hole until all the seeds are removed. Take care not to break through the skin.

# Dried Fruit Compote

| NUTRIENT ANALYSIS | |
|---|---|
| Calories | 154 |
| Protein | 1 g |
| Carbohydrate | 38 g |
| Total Fat | trace |
| Saturated Fat | 0 g |
| Cholesterol | 0 mg |
| Fiber | 3 g |
| Sugars | 5 g |
| Sodium | 12 mg |

Each serving counts as 1 fruit.

The high fiber content of dried fruits can assist with weight control while it also helps lower the risk of numerous life-compromising illnesses. I know I keep harping on the value of fiber, but it is an important food component for optimum health. If you desire, top each serving of this wonderful fruit compote with sugar-free, fat-free vanilla yogurt or frozen yogurt. You can purchase dried fruit in bulk at gourmet markets or at most health food stores.

**6 servings**

10 dried apricot halves, preferably the tart California variety
5 pitted prunes, halved
5 dried apple rings, cut into quarters
3 dried peach halves, cut into large chunks
2 dried figs, preferably black mission figs, stemmed and halved
3 cups unsweetened apple juice
¼ cup raisins
4 whole cloves
1 (4-inch) cinnamon stick
Zest of 1 lemon (*see* Note, page 101)

1. Combine all the ingredients in a large saucepan and bring to a simmer over medium-high heat. Cover, reduce heat to low, and continue simmering slowly until the fruit is soft, about 30 minutes. Remove the pan from the heat and allow the mixture to cool to room temperature, about 1 hour.

2. Transfer the mixture and any syrup in the pan to a large bowl. Cover tightly and store in the refrigerator up to 1 week. Discard the cinnamon stick and whole cloves before serving.

# Strawberry Sundaes

Who doesn't love an old-fashioned sundae for dessert? Try this light version, designed for a healthier diet with vitamin C–rich strawberries and guiltless frozen yogurt. This recipe can be easily doubled or tripled for parties or holiday gatherings.

**4 servings**

1 quart strawberries, hulled and cut into quarters
1/3 cup frozen unsweetened white grape–juice
    concentrate, thawed
1 tablespoon freshly squeezed lemon juice
Granulated sugar substitute equivalent to 1 tablespoon sugar
    (see product label)
1/4 teaspoon salt
1 pint sugar-free, fat-free vanilla frozen yogurt

1. Place the strawberries, white grape–juice concentrate, lemon juice, sugar substitute, and salt in a large saucepan set over high heat. Bring the mixture to a simmer, reduce the heat to low, and continue to simmer, uncovered, until somewhat thickened to the consistency of a loose jam, about 15 minutes. Transfer the mixture to a medium bowl and cool to room temperature, about 1 hour. Cover and store in the refrigerator up to 1 week.

2. Just before serving, place 1/2 cup frozen yogurt in each of 4 serving bowls and top each serving with 1/4 of the topping (a little less than 1 cup).

# Cherry Lime Rickey Gelatin Mold

**NUTRIENT ANALYSIS**

| | |
|---|---|
| Calories | 138 |
| Protein | 4 g |
| Carbohydrate | 30 g |
| Total Fat | 1 g |
| Saturated Fat | 0 g |
| Cholesterol | 1 g |
| Fiber | 1 g |
| Sugars | 0 g |
| Sodium | 76 mg |

Each serving counts as 1 fruit. There is also a negligible amount of low-fat dairy in this recipe.

Based on an old-fashioned soda fountain favorite, this fruit dessert can be made in advance so that it's ready when you are— perfect for those busy days when you literally may not have much time for lengthy meal preparation. This recipe can easily be doubled but, if you do that, be sure to use a two-quart gelatin mold.

**4 servings**

1 (.3-ounce) package sugar-free lime gelatin
1 cup boiling water
1 cup sugar-free lemon-lime soda
1$\frac{1}{2}$ cups canned pitted sweet cherries (unsweetened), drained; or 1$\frac{1}{2}$ cups frozen pitted sweet cherries (unsweetened), thawed
$\frac{1}{2}$ cup sugar-free, fat-free cherry yogurt
2 teaspoons grated lime zest (*see* Note, page 101)

1. Place the gelatin in a large bowl, pour in the boiling water, and stir until dissolved. Stir in the lemon-lime soda and refrigerate until slightly thickened, about 1 hour.

2. Stir in the cherries, pour the mixture into a 4-cup gelatin mold, and refrigerate until set, about 2 more hours.

3. Serve each portion with 2 tablespoons cherry yogurt and $\frac{1}{2}$ teaspoon grated lime zest spooned and sprinkled over the top.

# Holidays and Special Occasions

Now it is time to talk specifically about holidays, parties, and other special occasions—those eat-drink-and-be-merry times when you are most vulnerable to pushing your weight loss priorities off the list and suspending all the rules, because you tell yourself it's okay to indulge. For one thing, it's a fact that we do tend to put on extra pounds during the holidays. There is, however, both good news and bad news embedded in that statement. First, the good news: A recent study conducted by the National Institutes of Health (NIH) has found that people generally tend to gain just slightly over one pound between Thanksgiving and New Year's Day. So you may not gain as much weight over the holidays as you think you do. The bad news: According to that same study, if you don't take measures to avoid holiday weight gain, the extra weight does not drop away during the year but tends to accumulate over time and can be a major contributor to obesity.

Staying the course during holidays and special occasions can be a challenge unless you have a strategy in place to deal with the circumstances. What you can alter is the manner in which you prepare holiday and party meals, and this can be as simple as modifying recipes by using low-fat or sugar-free substitutes for otherwise fattening ingredients. Let this chapter be your guide. Here you will discover delicious ways to cook and a number of spectacular menus to smooth your journey through these often-tempting times, and, most important of all, let you enjoy your traditions and the occasions that bring together the people you love.

# Curried Tofu Dip

| NUTRIENT ANALYSIS | |
| --- | --- |
| Calories | 37 |
| Protein | 4 g |
| Carbohydrate | 4 g |
| Total Fat | 1 g |
| Saturated Fat | trace |
| Cholesterol | 1 mg |
| Fiber | trace |
| Sugars | 1 g |
| Sodium | 197 mg |

Each serving counts as a very small portion (about ⅛) of vegetarian protein.

Whether served for entertaining or just for snacking, this tangy almost fat-free dip is nutritious and full of flavor. Serve it with cut-up veggies or fat-free whole-wheat pita bread triangles.

**8 servings**

1 (12.3-ounce) package silken extra-firm light tofu, cut into chunks
½ cup fat-free sour cream or fat-free plain yogurt
2 tablespoons frozen apple- or pineapple-juice concentrate, thawed
1 tablespoon curry powder
1 teaspoon freshly squeezed lemon juice
½ teaspoon salt

1. Combine all the ingredients in a large blender or a food processor fitted with the chopping blade. Blend or process until creamy, about 1 minute, scraping down the sides of the container as necessary.

2. Spoon into a serving bowl and serve at once, or cover and refrigerate up to 3 days (allow to come back to room temperature before serving).

Grilled Greek Lamb Chops, page 112, and Asparagus with a Warm Vinaigrette, page 157.

Halibut Baked in Packets, page 127.

Italian Roast Pork Loin, page 106, and Roasted Beets, page 155.

Beef and Broccoli Stir-Fry, page 100.

Southern Oven-Fried Chicken, page 118, and Radish Slaw, page 154.

Mocha Fudge Pudding, page 184.

Banana Cream Pie, page 176.

Poached Pears, page 188.

# Orange-Glazed Turkey Breast

**NUTRIENT ANALYSIS**

| | |
|---|---:|
| Calories | 167 |
| Protein | 29 g |
| Carbohydrate | 10 g |
| Total Fat | 5 g |
| Saturated Fat | trace |
| Cholesterol | 48 mg |
| Fiber | 0 g |
| Sugars | 0 g |
| Sodium | 147 mg |

Each serving counts as 1 protein.

When you want to celebrate Thanksgiving—or any other holiday—without all the traditional fat and calories but with all the traditional trimmings, you've come to the right place. This baked turkey breast, glazed with a rich-tasting sauce, is the perfect holiday entrée for helping you stay true to your weight-management goals.

**10 servings**

$\frac{1}{2}$ cup no-salt, fat-free chicken broth, plus more as needed
$\frac{1}{2}$ cup sugar-free orange marmalade
1 tablespoon Dijon mustard
1 tablespoon reduced-sodium soy sauce
Nonstick spray, preferably olive-oil spray
1 (3-pound) tied skinless and boneless turkey breast roast
   (*see* Note)

1. Position a rack in the center of the oven and preheat to 325°F. Whisk the broth, marmalade, mustard, and soy sauce in a small saucepan set over medium heat. When the mixture comes to a simmer, cover the pan and set it aside off the heat.

2. Lightly coat a large nonstick skillet with spray and place it over medium-high heat. Brown the turkey roast on all sides, turning as necessary, about 5 minutes. Transfer the turkey to a roasting pan just large enough to hold it securely with a little room for the juices and sauce. Pour the warm broth mixture over the roast and cover the pan with aluminum foil.

3. Roast for 1 hour. Remove the foil and continue to roast, basting every 5 minutes with the pan juices, until golden brown,

(*continued on next page*)

Orange-Glazed Turkey Breast *(cont.)*

about 30 more minutes. An instant-read meat thermometer inserted into the thickest part of the roast should register 170°F. If the pan juices begin to dry up, add more broth as necessary. Let the roast stand at room temperature 5 minutes before removing the butcher twine and carving. If desired, skim any pan juices of fat and serve on the side.

**NOTE:** Turkey breast roasts are sometimes sold pretied but with the skin intact. If so, snip off the twine and remove the skin, then retie the roast with butcher twine. Tying the roast helps it keep its shape as it cooks. You can also ask the butcher at your local market to do this for you.

# Sausage Dressing

**NUTRIENT ANALYSIS**

| | |
|---|---|
| Calories | 142 |
| Protein | 13 g |
| Carbohydrate | 12 g |
| Total Fat | 5 g |
| Saturated Fat | trace |
| Cholesterol | 40 mg |
| Fiber | 2 g |
| Sugars | 0 g |
| Sodium | 755 mg |

Each serving counts as
1 nonstarchy vegetable,
½ starchy carbohydrate, and
a partial serving (2 ounces) of
protein.

Holiday dressing recipes are traditionally passed down from generation to generation, with very few variations. This one, with reduced saturated fat and calories, is an exception. We hope that you will use it to start a new tradition that celebrates good health during the holidays.

**8 servings**

Nonstick spray
1 pound lean turkey sausage, casings removed
1 medium onion, finely chopped
1 green bell pepper, cored, seeded, and chopped
1 garlic clove, minced
3 ribs celery, thinly sliced
6 ounces button mushrooms, brushed of any dirt and thinly
   sliced (about 3 ½ cups)
4 slices stale whole-wheat bread (*see* Note 1)
¾ cup no-salt, fat-free chicken broth
¼ cup pasteurized egg substitute
2 teaspoons rubbed sage
2 teaspoons dried thyme
1 teaspoon salt, or less, to taste
½ teaspoon freshly ground black pepper

1. Preheat oven to 325°F.

2. Spray a large nonstick skillet with nonstick spray and set over medium heat. Crumble in the sausage and cook, stirring often, until brown, about 3 minutes. Place the sausage and any pan juices in a colander set in the sink to drain.

*(continued on next page)*

Sausage Dressing *(cont.)*

3. Return the skillet to medium heat, add the onion, bell pepper, and garlic, and cook, stirring, until softened, about 2 minutes. Add the celery and cook 1 minute more, stirring often. Add the mushrooms and cook, stirring from time to time, until they give off their juice and it reduces to a glaze, leaving the pan nearly dry, about 5 minutes. Transfer the mixture to a large bowl and stir in the drained sausage, breaking it up to distribute it evenly among the vegetables.

4. Tear the bread slices into $1/2$-inch bits and stir into the bowl. Stir in the broth, egg substitute, sage, thyme, salt, and pepper (*see* Note 2).

5. Spray a 9 x 13–inch baking pan with nonstick spray and spoon in the dressing.

6. Bake until golden brown, about 40 minutes. Let stand 5 minutes before serving.

**NOTE 1:** Stale bread will not fall apart as quickly as fresh when moistened with the broth and vegetables. The night before making this recipe, simply leave the slices out, uncovered.

**NOTE 2:** If you like a sweeter dressing, also stir in $1/3$ cup raisins and 1 small tart apple, such as a Granny Smith, peeled, cored, and roughly chopped.

# Rosemary Mashed Potatoes

This true comfort food is transformed into a healthy side dish with the addition of fat-free sour cream or fat-free evaporated milk. Using fresh rosemary gives these mashed potatoes such a wonderful taste that you definitely won't miss the gravy.

**8 servings**

$\frac{2}{3}$ cup no-salt, fat-free chicken or vegetable broth
2 tablespoons fresh rosemary, chopped
6 large baking potatoes, preferably russet, peeled and cut into
    1-inch pieces
$\frac{1}{3}$ cup fat-free sour cream, at room temperature, or
    $\frac{1}{3}$ cup fat-free evaporated milk
2 teaspoons Dijon mustard
$\frac{1}{2}$ teaspoon salt
Sweet paprika or freshly ground black pepper, to taste

1. Place the broth and rosemary in a small saucepan set over high heat. Bring the mixture to a simmer, cover, remove from heat, and set aside.

2. Place the potatoes in a large saucepan and cover with cool water to a depth of 2 inches. Bring to a boil over high heat. Partially cover, reduce the heat to medium-low, and simmer until potatoes are tender, about 15 minutes. Drain.

3. Place the potatoes in a large bowl and mash with a potato masher or an electric mixer at medium speed. Beat in the rosemary and broth mixture, then beat in the sour cream or evaporated milk, mustard, and salt. Spoon into a medium bowl and garnish with the paprika or ground black pepper before serving.

# Roasted Vegetables

| NUTRIENT ANALYSIS | |
| --- | --- |
| Calories | 98 |
| Protein | 3 g |
| Carbohydrate | 15 g |
| Total Fat | 4 g |
| Saturated Fat | .5 g |
| Cholesterol | 0 mg |
| Fiber | 4 g |
| Sugars | 1 g |
| Sodium | 373 mg |

Each serving counts as
1 nonstarchy vegetable.

Roasting brings out the best in these nutrition-packed vegetables. Because they appeal to everyone, roasted vegetables make the perfect side dish for holiday parties. Prepare a heap of them and place them on your buffet table so your guests can help themselves.

**8 servings**

1 large rutabaga, peeled and cut into 1-inch cubes
1 large turnip, peeled and cut into 1-inch cubes
2 cups baby carrots
2 cups small Brussels sprouts (*see* Note 1)
2 tablespoons olive oil
1 teaspoon salt
$1/2$ teaspoon freshly ground black pepper
3 tablespoons sugar-free maple syrup

1. Preheat the oven to 400°F.

2. Combine the rutabaga, turnip, carrots, and Brussels sprouts in a large bowl and toss with the olive oil, salt, and pepper. Transfer to a roasting or broiler pan. Use a rubber spatula to scrape the bowl clean of any remaining oil, salt, and pepper; drizzle it over the vegetables.

3. Roast, tossing every 10 minutes or so to prevent sticking, until golden brown and tender, about 1 hour and 10 minutes.

4. Pour the maple syrup into the hot roasting pan and toss with the roasted vegetables (*see* Note 2). Pour the entire mixture into a serving bowl and drizzle any remaining pan juices over the vegetables.

**NOTE 1:** For accurate and even cooking, make a small "x" with a paring knife in the stem end of each Brussels sprout.

**NOTE 2:** If you want a sweet-and-sour dressing, add 1 tablespoon cider vinegar to the oil, and drizzle over the hot vegetables.

# Shrimp and Artichoke Appetizers

| NUTRIENT ANALYSIS | |
|---|---|
| Calories | 69 |
| Protein | 6 g |
| Carbohydrate | 9 g |
| Total Fat | trace |
| Saturated Fat | 0 g |
| Cholesterol | 18 mg |
| Fiber | 3 g |
| Sugars | 0 g |
| Sodium | 288 mg |

Each serving counts as
1 nonstarchy vegetable.
There is also a negligible
amount of protein in this recipe.

These imaginative and innovative appetizers are very easy to fix for parties and can be prepared ahead of time so that you avoid any last-minute rush. The recipe can be doubled or tripled for crowds.

**6 servings**

1¼ teaspoons prepared wasabi paste (*see* Note 2)
12 canned artichoke bottoms packed in water, drained and
    rinsed (*see* Note 1)
12 medium cooked, peeled, and deveined cocktail shrimp
    (about ½ pound)
Twelve strips nori (dried Japanese seaweed), cut into strips
    8½ inches long by ½ inch wide (*see* Note 2)
3 teaspoons rice vinegar or white wine vinegar (*see* Note 2)

1. Spread a scant ¼ teaspoon wasabi on top of each artichoke bottom and top with a shrimp.

2. Dampen one end of one of the nori strips and wrap around the artichoke bottom and the shrimp, pressing the ends together to seal them so that the nori holds the shrimp in place. Sprinkle

*(continued on next page)*

Shrimp and Artichoke Appetizers *(cont.)*

¼ teaspoon vinegar over the top and repeat with the remaining ingredients. Serve immediately.

**NOTE 1:** Use the flat artichoke bottoms, not the more familiar artichoke hearts. The bottoms are often found with the Italian foods in grocery stores or supermarkets.

**NOTE 2:** Several of the ingredients in this recipe may be unfamiliar to you. Wasabi paste is made from the mashed root of Japanese horseradish. Nori strips are made from dried seaweed formed into paper-thin sheets. Rice vinegar is a clear vinegar made from glutinous rice. All three can be found in all Asian markets, almost all health food stores, most gourmet markets, and in the Asian section of some supermarkets.

# Easter Lamb with Mint Pesto

**NUTRIENT ANALYSIS**

| | |
|---|---|
| Calories | 259 |
| Protein | 36 g |
| Carbohydrate | 2 g |
| Total Fat | 11 g |
| Saturated Fat | 4 g |
| Cholesterol | 110 mg |
| Fiber | .5 |
| Sugars | 0 g |
| Sodium | 382 mg |

Each serving counts as 1 protein.

Serving lamb as a lean protein source is a smart move, since it is high in B vitamins, iron, and zinc, as well as surprisingly low in calories. Here lamb is rubbed with a special herb paste that accentuates and enhances the delicate flavor of the meat. This recipe makes a perfect Easter or special-occasion meal for family or guests.

**8 servings**

2 garlic cloves, quartered
1 cup packed fresh mint leaves
1 cup packed fresh basil leaves
1/2 cup water
3 tablespoons sliced almonds
2 teaspoons grated lemon zest (*see* Note, page 101)
1 teaspoon salt
1/2 teaspoon freshly ground black pepper
1 (3-pound) boneless leg of lamb, butterflied
    (about 1/2 a leg, *see* Note 1)
Butcher twine

1. Position a rack in the center of the oven and preheat to 350°F.

2. Place all the ingredients except the lamb in a blender or a food processor fitted with the chopping blade and blend or process, scraping down the sides of the container as necessary, until somewhat smooth if still a little grainy, about 1 minute.

3. Lay the boneless leg of lamb out on a work surface and rub the cut (or rough) side with the pesto mixture, spreading it evenly across the meat and massaging it in just a bit. Roll the leg of lamb

*(continued on next page)*

Easter Lamb with Mint Pesto *(cont.)*

into a meatloaf-sized bundle, tying it with butcher twine in two or three places to secure it closed, particularly at the ends.

4. Place the lamb in a shallow roasting pan or a broiler pan and roast until an instant-read meat thermometer inserted into the thickest part of the meat registers 140°F for medium-rare or 155°F for medium (*see* Note 2). Remove the roast from the oven, tent it with foil, and let it stand at room temperature for 5 minutes. Snip off the butcher twine and carve.

**NOTE 1:** Boneless leg of lamb is often sold butterflied and tied. If yours is not butterflied (i.e., splayed open to show the most surface area), have the butcher in your market do it for you, but don't have him tie it up. He can sell you the twine to tie it up when you get home, or you can buy butcher twine at most hardware stores. Do not use colored thread, which has dyes that are not necessarily edible and can bleed into the meat.

**NOTE 2:** If you don't want to go to the trouble of tying the roast, you can simply broil it. To do so, do not coat the lamb with the pesto mixture. Instead, heat the broiler and spray a broiler pan with nonstick spray. Sprinkle 1 teaspoon salt, $1/2$ teaspoon freshly ground pepper, and the juice of 2 lemons over the meat. Lay the butterflied leg of lamb on the pan, cut (or rough) side up, position it about 6 inches from the heat source, and broil 10 minutes. Turn it over and broil another 12 minutes, or until the internal temperature registers as indicated in the recipe. Serve the mint pesto on the side.

# Steamed Whole Red Snapper

| NUTRIENT ANALYSIS | |
| --- | --- |
| Calories | 293 |
| Protein | 61 g |
| Carbohydrate | 3 g |
| Total Fat | 4 g |
| Saturated Fat | trace |
| Cholesterol | 168 mg |
| Fiber | 1 g |
| Sugars | 1 g |
| Sodium | 594 mg |

Each serving counts as 1 protein.

This savory steamed red snapper is an impressive dish when served as a party entrée. Keep this health fact in mind, too: If you eat fish at least once a week, you can help lower your blood pressure, triglycerides, and cholesterol, thus reducing your risk of heart disease.

### 4 servings

1 (4-pound) whole red snapper, skin scored in 3 places on each
    side (*see* Note 1)
1/2 cup packed fresh cilantro leaves
3 scallions, white and green parts, cut in 2-inch pieces
1/4 cup peeled and chopped fresh ginger (*see* Note, page 101)
2 tablespoons reduced-sodium soy sauce
1 tablespoon rice vinegar or white wine vinegar
1 teaspoon toasted sesame oil

1. Place 1 inch water in a large Dutch oven. Remove the tops and bottoms from two well-scrubbed empty tuna cans (leaving just the ring) and place in the Dutch oven. Or cut a large raw baking potato into three 2-inch-thick rings and place them in the Dutch oven.

2. Place the fish on a heat-safe plate that will fit comfortably in the Dutch oven—trim the tail to fit if necessary, but the head can lap a little over the side. Stuff the cilantro leaves in the belly and sprinkle the scallions and ginger over the top of the fish. Stand the plate on the cans or the potato rings in the Dutch oven.

*(continued on next page)*

Steamed Whole Red Snapper *(cont.)*

3. Place the Dutch oven over medium-high heat and bring the water to a simmer. Cover the pot and steam the fish until tender, about 10 minutes. Remove from heat and let the pot stand, covered, for 5 minutes.

4. Using oven mitts to protect your hands, remove the plate from the pot. Drain any liquid from the plate, sprinkle the fish with the soy sauce, vinegar, and sesame oil, and serve at once (*see* Note 2), with a spoonful of herbs and any sauce on the plate.

**NOTE 1:** There are two rules for buying fresh fish. First, smell it. It should smell clean and bright. Second, check the eyes. They should be clear and bright, not cloudy. Blood spots are fine if they are bright red, not coagulated and dark.

**NOTE 2:** The easiest way to serve this fish is right on the plate that served as its steamer. To serve, first use a large knife to make a long cut down one side of the body right where the backbone lies (that is, about 1/2 inch from the top of the fish, were it swimming in the water). Do not cut through the backbone. Next, make a horizontal cut along the top of the fish down to the backbone and remove the back and the dorsal fins, which are attached to it. Slip a large fork or a thin spatula under the meat and lift the top fillet off the bones, dividing it in two sections for two servings. Remove the bones by pulling up the tail and zipping the backbone and all attached bones from the bottom fillet, thereby also pulling the head loose from the fish. Divide the bottom fillet in half for two servings. Warmed dinner plates at the table are a nice way to keep the fish hot until it's eaten.

# Broccoli Soufflé

**NUTRIENT ANALYSIS**

| | |
|---|---|
| Calories | 125 |
| Protein | 12 g |
| Carbohydrate | 13 g |
| Total Fat | 3 g |
| Saturated Fat | 1 g |
| Cholesterol | 114 mg |
| Fiber | 1 g |
| Sugars | 0 g |
| Sodium | 482 mg |

Each serving counts as
1 nonstarchy vegetable and
½ low-fat dairy product. Each
serving also counts as 1 egg, so
be sure to take that into
consideration if you are watching
your egg intake for the week.

Although it makes an excellent presentation at a dinner party, this tasty and nutritious broccoli soufflé is also a great choice for a casual brunch or lunch. Try serving it with a salad of fresh fruit or tossed greens for a complete meal, or pair it with any one of the main dishes in this cookbook.

**4 servings**

Nonstick spray
2 large egg yolks
½ pound frozen broccoli florets, thawed
1 teaspoon salt
½ teaspoon freshly ground black pepper
¼ teaspoon freshly grated or ground nutmeg
   (*see* Note, page 129)
2 cups fat-free milk
2 tablespoons whole-wheat flour
4 large egg whites

1. Position a rack in the center of the oven and preheat to 375°F. Spray an 8-cup soufflé dish or high-sided round casserole with nonstick spray and set it aside. Place the egg yolks in a medium bowl, whisk lightly, and set aside.

2. Place the broccoli in a food processor fitted with the chopping blade or in a large blender and process or blend until fairly smooth. Mix in the salt, pepper, and nutmeg and set aside.

3. Bring 1½ cups of the milk to a low simmer in a large saucepan set over medium-high heat. Meanwhile, whisk the remaining ½ cup milk and the whole-wheat flour in a small bowl until

(*continued on next page*)

Broccoli Soufflé *(cont.)*

smooth. Whisk the flour mixture into the hot milk, and continue to heat, whisking constantly, until simmering and thickened, about 20 seconds.

4. Whisk $1/2$ the hot milk mixture into the egg yolks, then whisk this egg mixture back into the pan with the remaining milk mixture. Cook for 10 seconds. Immediately remove the pan from the heat and stir in the broccoli puree. Transfer the mixture to a large bowl and set aside for 5 minutes.

5. With an electric mixer at high speed, beat the egg whites in a large clean bowl until stiff peaks form.

6. Using a wooden spoon or a rubber spatula, stir half the beaten egg whites into the broccoli mixture. Then fold in the remaining egg whites using long even arcs so as not to deflate the egg whites. Fold just until incorporated—there will still be white streaks in the batter. Gently transfer the mixture to the prepared soufflé dish or casserole.

7. Bake until puffed and lightly browned, about 45 minutes. Serve at once.

# Festive Fruit Punch

| NUTRIENT ANALYSIS | |
| --- | ---: |
| Calories | 130 |
| Protein | 1 g |
| Carbohydrate | 32 g |
| Total Fat | 0 g |
| Saturated Fat | 0 g |
| Cholesterol | 0 mg |
| Fiber | .5 |
| Sugars | 0 |
| Sodium | 7 mg |

Each serving counts as 1¼ fruits.

This cool and refreshing punch is perfect for summer parties and get-togethers. Serve it as a healthy replacement for alcohol, which interferes with your body's ability to burn fat efficiently and should be avoided as you shed pounds.

**16 servings**

4 cups unsweetened white grape juice
1 (15-ounce) can frozen unsweetened pineapple-juice
        concentrate, thawed
1 (15-ounce) can frozen unsweetened orange-juice
        concentrate, thawed
2 (1-liter) bottles sugar-free raspberry seltzer (preferably clear.)

1. Pour the white grape juice into ice cube trays (*see* Note) and freeze, at least 4 hours or overnight.

2. Combine the pineapple- and orange-juice concentrates and seltzer in a large punch bowl. Add the grape juice ice cubes and serve at once. (If no punch bowl is available, serve in large pitchers.)

**NOTE:** If you chill the white grape juice first, it will yield clearer ice cubes that are less resistant to shattering. For an extrafancy presentation, place 1 raspberry in each ice cube compartment before adding the white grape juice. Each cube will then have a little jewel-like raspberry in its center.

# Mulled "Cider"

**NUTRIENT ANALYSIS**

| | |
|---|---|
| Calories | 148 |
| Protein | .5 g |
| Carbohydrate | 35 g |
| Total Fat | trace |
| Saturated Fat | 0 g |
| Cholesterol | 0 g |
| Fiber | 2 g |
| Sugars | trace |
| Sodium | 7 mg |

Each serving counts as 1 fruit.

Gather around the fireplace with a warm mug of this mulled cider, seasoned with cloves, cinnamon, and nutmeg. Sip it slowly for a filling, satisfying winter drink. Double or triple the recipe when you have a houseful of guests.

**4 servings**

2 oranges
1 tablespoon whole cloves
1 quart unsweetened apple juice
2 (4-inch) cinnamon sticks
$\frac{1}{2}$ teaspoon rum extract, optional
Freshly grated or ground nutmeg, optional (*see* Note, page 129)

1. Stud the oranges with whole cloves, then cut the oranges into quarters. Place the orange quarters, apple juice, cinnamon sticks, and rum extract, if using, in a large saucepan set over medium-high heat and bring to a boil. Cover, reduce the heat to low, and simmer 10 minutes.

2. Remove the orange sections, with their cloves and the cinnamon sticks. Ladle the cider into mugs and top each serving with a dash of nutmeg, if desired. Serve at once.

# Spiced Tea

Some of the most meaningful gift-giving can start in your very own kitchen with delicious recipes like this spiced tea. This special mixture can be made in quantity and packed into decorative jars for gifts your family and friends will cherish. Buy tea in bulk at warehouse discount stores.

1 pound loose black tea leaves, such as Prince of Wales, Oolong, Ceylon, Darjeeling, English Breakfast, or Irish Breakfast, regular or decaffeinated
1 tablespoon whole cloves
2 tablespoons dried orange peel (*see* Note, page 165)
10 cardamom pods
3 (4-inch) cinnamon sticks, crumbled into small shards

Combine all the ingredients in a large bowl or a metal tin with a lid and store, tightly covered, in a cool, dark place. Scoop out as much as you need at any time, either for a single cup of tea (1 teaspoon of the tea blend yields about 1 cup tea) or to package in decorative jars or tins to give as gifts.

# Provençal Vinegar

During the holidays, there is no hard-and-fast rule that says you must bake cookies or make candy as gifts (and thus put yourself in the potentially tempting position of wolfing down most of what you fix). Instead, try something different, such as this wonderfully flavored vinegar. It can be drizzled over any salad, steamed or roasted vegetables, or even roasted or grilled beef, lamb, or pork. Make the vinegar several months before a holiday or keep some on hand to give as birthday gifts. You can use any kind of jar, from canning jars and lids to the fancy glass bottles sold at craft stores, or even a washed empty ketchup bottle with the label removed! You can buy the vinegar in bulk at most outlet warehouse stores.

Per bottle
1 whole lemon
4 thyme branches
4 allspice berries
2 rosemary stalks
2 bay leaves
3 garlic cloves
White wine or red wine vinegar to fill bottle

1. Remove the zest from the lemon with a vegetable peeler and cut into long strips. (Wrap and refrigerate the lemon flesh for another use.)

2. Place the herbs, garlic, and zest in a Mason jar, canning jar, or other decorative bottle, and fill with the vinegar, leaving a $1/2$-inch space at the top. Seal and place in a cool, dark place at least 2 weeks or up to 6 months.

# Epilogue

This cookbook has been my effort to help you find new and better ways to prepare food so that you can get down to a healthy weight and keep yourself there. If you've read through this book and tried the recipes and cooking techniques I've offered, you now have some valuable tools to do something positive for your health. Immerse yourself in these tools and techniques. Make them a part of the way you cook, nourish yourself and family, and rebuild your own health and vitality.

Remember that you are on the road to changing, reprogramming, and strategizing your life to achieve what you want. When you begin to make even the most gradual adjustments in how you eat and cook, your weight will begin to change and you will go a long way toward protecting yourself against some very real health problems.

You can start with our recipes, adapt them, and even add some of your own. Experiment. Be creative. Have fun, because eating for health does not cancel out eating for pleasure. The more new foods you try, the more satisfying, successful, and enjoyable your journey to weight loss freedom will be. And you'll go a long way toward creating the experience of health and well-being that has eluded you until now.

Each time you make smart food choices, each time you prepare recipes of nutritional merit, each time you decide to live with health and well-being, you will become stronger, and the next smart choice and healthy decision will become that much easier to make. You yourself will be the greatest beneficiary of this positive change, and the life you've been living will be transformed for the better.

With yourself as the focus of your efforts to change, and using the seven keys to weight loss freedom, you will promote the life you want to have, and you will become the fit, healthy person you are capable of being. Keep going, and give it your best. You're worth it.

# Liquid Measure
## Cups, quarts, ounces, pounds, and their metric equivalents

CONVERSION FORMULAS: To convert: *Quarts to liters,* multiply the quarts by 0.94635; *Liters into quarts,* multiply the liters by 1.056688; *Ounces into milliliters,* multiply the ounces by 29.573; *Milliliters into ounces,* multiply the milliliters by 0.0338.

Nearest convenient equivalents (with nearest actual equivalents in parentheses)

| Cups and Spoons | Quarts and Ounces | Metric Equivalents |
|---|---|---|
| **4⅓ cups** | 1 quart 2 ounces (1.056 quarts) | 1 liter 1,000 milliliters |
| **4 cups** | 1 quart | 1 liter less 1 deciliter (0.946 liter) |
| **2 cups (plus 2½ Tb)** | 17 ounces (16.907 ounces) | ½ liter |
| **2 cups** | 1 pint; 16 ounces | ½ liter less 1½ Tb (0.473 liter) |
| **1 cup (plus 1¼ Tb)** | 8 ounces (8.454 ounces) | ¼ liter |
| **1 cup** | 8 ounces | ¼ liter (0.236 liter) |
| **⅓ cup (plus 1 Tb)** | 3½ ounces (3.381 ounces) | 1 deciliter ⅒ liter 100 milliliters |
| **⅓ cup** | 2⅔ ounces | 1 deciliter less 1⅓ Tb (0.079 liter) |
| **3⅓ Tb** | 1¾ ounces (1.690 ounces) | ½ deciliter 50 milliliters |
| **1 Tb** | ½ ounce | 15 milliliters 15 grams |
| **2 tsp** | ⅓ ounce | 10 milliliters 10 grams |
| **1 tsp** | ⅒ ounce | 5 milliliters 5 grams |

# American Oven Temperatures vs. Centigrade

| Fahrenheit Degrees | Centigrade Degrees |
|---|---|
| 160 | 71 |
| 212 | 100 |
| 221 | 105 |
| 225 | 107 |
| 230 | 121 |
| 300 | 149 |
| 302 | 150 |
| 350 | 177 |
| 375 | 190 |
| 400 | 205 |
| 425 | 218 |
| 475 | 246 |
| 500 | 260 |
| 525 | 274 |
| 550 | 288 |

# Weights

CONVERSION FORMULAS: To convert: *Ounces into grams,* multiply the ounces by 28.3495; *Grams into ounces,* multiply the grams by 0.35274.

| Pounds and Ounces (most convenient approximation) | Metric |
|---|---|
| 2.2 pounds | 1 kilogram 1,000 grams |
| 1.1 pounds | 500 grams |
| 1 pound (16 ounces) | 464 grams |
| 9 ounces | 250 grams |
| ½ pound (8 ounces) | 227 grams |
| 4⅜ ounces | 125 grams |
| ¼ pound (4 ounces) | 114 grams |
| 3½ ounces | 100 grams |
| 2⅔ ounces | 75 grams |
| 1¾ ounces | 50 grams |
| 1 ounce | 30 grams (28.3 gr.) |
| 1 scant ounce | 25 grams |
| ½ ounce | 15 grams |
| ⅓ ounce | 10 grams |
| ⅙ ounce | 5 grams |

# Index

# About the Author

Dr. Phil McGraw is the #1 *New York Times* bestselling author of *The Ultimate Weight Solution, Self Matters, Life Strategies,* and *Relationship Rescue.* He is the host of the nationally syndicated, daily one-hour series *Dr. Phil.* One of the world's foremost experts in the field of human functioning, Dr. McGraw is the cofounder of Courtroom Sciences, Inc., the world's leading litigation consulting firm. Dr. McGraw currently lives in Los Angeles, California, with his wife and two sons.